Water Under the Bridge

To Arthur, a kind and
caring cousin-in-law.
With best wishes,
Jean

Water Under the Bridge

Part One
The Early Years

Pamela Jean Heyman

Library of Congress Control Number:		2010916363
ISBN:	Hardcover	978-1-4568-0951-5
	Softcover	978-1-4568-0950-8
	Ebook	978-1-4568-0952-2

This book was printed in the United States of America.

To order additional copies of this book, contact:
Xlibris Corporation
0-800-644-6988
www.xlibrispublishing.co.uk
Orders@xlibrispublishing.co.uk
300853

Part One
(1931-1956)

Contents

Addendums

Copies of references from the North Central School and K&J.

Photographs.

Dedication

With profound gratitude to my grandmother and
Aunty Kalla for always being there through the bad times
and providing so many of the good times.

Foreword

When I retired, I had stated my intention of writing a book about my life, and this intention was reinforced by subsequent events. After the deaths of my mother and then Bert, whenever we had a family get-together, Barclay, my middle brother, would get very upset when we talked about the past; he felt quite excluded from the memories which Peter, Maureen, and I, and to some extent Chris, shared. And so, Barclay, I have written this first part for you, to help you to understand what went before.

Thankfully, we have always remained close brothers and sisters, and with the advancing years, we have kept in contact, our meetings usually orchestrated by Chris but sadly, within the past four years, without Peter and Maureen, who have gone on ahead. Circumstances do not always allow for it, but it emphasizes how important it is to remember together the significance of family ties and how they have evolved.

I would also like to clarify that my recollections of having been told as a child that my great-grandfather was Sir Peter Heyman was wildly out date wise. Another activity I have pursued was to trace my family tree; Sir Peter Heyman, according to my research, was born in 1580 and died in 1641. I have been unable to trace my antecedents back to anywhere near that date, but hey, my surname was Heyman as a single girl!

So now to the important part—to thank all those who have encouraged and helped me with getting *Water Under the Bridge* published. First, it has to be my husband's cousin, Mair, who convinced me to send the manuscript to publishers, even providing me with an address. When it was accepted, I could not believe that something that I had written for the family was considered a book of considerable merit. Mair, many many thanks. Then to my good friend Rowena, who proofread in the early stages and whose help was invaluable. To my brother, Chris, who assisted me greatly with advice and the production of copies of the manuscript. To Bob (Robert

Lovell), whose technical assistance throughout has been incalculable and who brought me to the finale with his production of the cover design. Your generosity in devoting so much time to achieving such a perfect result is beyond words. Then last, but certainly not least, to my husband, John, and all my family and friends who have supported me in this venture. Without this *Water Under the Bridge* may well not have seen the light of day.

Park Farm, Throwley, Kent

This was the home of my grandparents, Walter and (Annie) Maude Hooker. The property was leased from a local large estate owner, whom I later understood to be Earl Sondes. It was a large farm—arable and stock—and the farmhouse and farm buildings stood in the centre of the land—on a crossroads approached by a drive called The Larches. Of the other three fingers of the crossroads, one extended to the village of Throwley, the second to Belmont, and the third to the farmhands' cottages that overlooked a valley referred to as the 'bottoms'. Approaching the farm up The Larches, one came first to the two cherry orchards on the left-hand side with a large wooden shed in the corner, which housed all the sacks of grain—and cherry-picking baskets and boxes. The old orchard on the right had a large piggery and, at one time, the ferret cages. This approach brought one to the back of the farmhouse, which was surrounded by a fenced-off garden. A high brick wall separated the garden from the farmyard, and the stables, cowsheds, barn, and other outbuildings formed a square behind this.

Like most farmhouses, the front door of Park Farm was rarely used, and so the entrance was always by the back door, guarded by a grating to scrape off the mud from muddy shoes or boots. It led into a passageway which had three doors—the first one on the left into the dairy, immediately ahead into the scullery/kitchen and on the right into the living room. A door from the living room went into the front hall; on the left, a door opened on to the staircase to the bedrooms, to the right a further door to the 'big room' and, of course, the front door. The staircase led on to a large landing and four bedrooms. There was no lighting other than oil lamps in the living rooms and kitchen and candlesticks in the bedrooms, no inside toilet and certainly no heating other than fireplaces in all rooms.

In the kitchen, the water supply was hand pumped into a glazed earthenware sink that stood under the window. Water was heated in the copper, under which a fire was lit on washing day (Monday) and bath night (Friday), and the water to fill the copper had to be pumped into buckets in the sink and then carried the short distance to the copper. Inevitably, there were spills and the uneven surface of the bare brick floor developed puddles. In the opposite corner to the copper was the large black kitchen range, as it was called. This was the heart of the house, where all the cooking took place. The fire was never allowed to go out; kettles always stood on the flat top as another source of hot water. There was a large, scrubbed top table in the centre of the kitchen, two comfortable wooden chairs on either side of the range, and a clothes rack hanging from the ceiling, where clothes were aired after pressing. It was always a scene of such activity—when specific days were allocated for baking, pressing, cleaning, butter making, and bread making.

Both my mother (Marjorie Jean) and her sister (Kathleen Mary but nicknamed Kalla) were born and brought up here. They both attended Faversham Grammar School as fee-paying pupils. My grandmother often recounted how she would scrimp and save for those fees by selling eggs and butter in Faversham market—often walking a distance of eighteen miles there and back to do that in the days of the recession.

My mother—at the age of eighteen—married a local man called Ernest Cooper Heyman. His parents had a bakery business and cafe in Faversham but lived in a property not far from Park Farm in Throwley. As I understand it, my parents never set up their own home, but lived mainly with either my grandparents at Park Farm or with my father's parents. And it was at Park Farm that I was born on 8 January 1931 followed some two years later by my brother, Peter (William Cooper Heyman). The marriage of my parents broke up soon after Peter's arrival, and neither of us have any memory of our father, only the hearsay that we occasionally picked up—that he had always been a bit of ladies' man and had finally met and married someone older than himself with quite a bit of money. Therefore, my early memories of life at Park Farm are of my grandparents, and particularly of my grandmother, because after the end of the marriage and subsequent divorce, my mother went to live in Maidstone where she trained and then worked as a hairdresser.

Aunty Kalla became a teacher and initially was living and teaching in the village of Appledore in Kent. However, when I was about three, she returned to Park Farm and, apart from a period of about a year, when she took me with her to live at the vicarage, she managed the farm because of my grandfather's failing health.

It is against this background that my early formative years were spent. Memories of breakfast in the living room around the table with Grandad, who had a habit of cutting his bread and butter (spread liberally with butter and marmalade) into squares and the only cat who lived indoors, sitting on his shoulder, being given the occasional 'square', which he ate very fastidiously. At one stage, a teacher from the village school lodged with us, and she had the treat of half a grapefruit before the main breakfast—something of which I was very envious. During better weather, I can remember mid-morning partaking of bread and cheese with Grandad, sitting on the well cover in the garden. Somehow, Grandad's food always tasted better than my own—my mouth still waters when I think about it! Dinner was always at midday—Grandad would go out shooting and return with a rabbit or two, which Grandma turned into a delicious rabbit pie. During the week, tea was an equally delicious meal of home-made butter, jams, bread, cakes, which was dressed up with further goodies such as trifles and cold meats on Sundays.

My grandmother worked hard, looking after us all. She had two large chicken huts in the orchard, and there was always a plentiful supply of fresh eggs and the occasional chicken, which reached the dinner table eventually. Both Peter and I would help her to feed the chicken and collect the eggs. There were also the orphaned lambs to cope with during the lambing season when they had to be fed with milk from bottles with a teat. What a feat it was to keep the teat on the bottle as the lambs sucked with such force that quite often the bottle and teat came apart and the milk was spilled.

One of my early memories is cherry picking time; Grandad would bring in families of cockneys, who lived in huts at the top of the orchard and picked the cherries. They cooked their food and boiled their billycans on open wood fires, and there was always a plentiful supply of stewed, wood smoked, tea on hand. There were always a number of children who, whilst we were not allowed to play with them, always proved of great interest since they were allowed to go up the ladders into the cherry trees and stayed up until late hours around the campfire with their elders. And they were allowed to have dirty faces and dirty clothes! I suppose the mind tends to enhance one's memories of childhood, but somehow the sun always seemed to be shining and the weather to be warm, other than one particular winter that stands out when the snow was really heavy. I went to school because Aunty Kalla was teaching there and, against her better judgement, Grandma allowed me to accompany her. I arrived at school with my Wellingtons full of snow that had come over the tops when I had gone through the drifts, and we very soon did the return journey of about three-quarters of a mile to thaw out and dry off. The school was closed for about three days.

Peter was a great favourite with everyone—he was always a very happy and placid child. He was also a grandson—Grandma had always wanted a boy but had two girls, and with Peter's birth, she got her wish. Not that I was in any way thought less of—but somehow he took pride of place; when we had visitors, it was Peter who had to stand up and recite, and I remember feeling quite resentful that my own ability to do likewise was ignored! In actual fact, Peter and I were not a close brother and sister during our early years—I remember that we did quarrel quite a bit, and our activities seemed to keep us apart. Peter had a huge collection of small cars that he would line up on the pattern of the chenille tablecloth on the large table in the living room, and he would be very content to play with those for hours. I was not allowed to touch them!

We usually accompanied Grandma and Aunty Kalla to the Women's Institute and Mother's union meetings (Aunty Kalla was secretary/treasurer and Grandma was chair). We had to play quietly in the back of the hall during the winter or outside during better weather. Peter would be dressed up in shantung suits and white shoes and socks whilst I, although perfectly respectably attired, would not be quite so appreciative of the impression I created! Aunty Kalla was usually the one who took us shopping for clothes, and she had very conservative taste. I particularly remember her buying me a new winter coat, which, of course, only came out on high days and holidays. It was Harris Tweed in an uninteresting colour and, horror of horrors, it was a boy's coat that fastened on the wrong side for a girl. But it was quality! How I hated that coat! My mother, grandmother, and aunty Kalla were excellent knitters and produced jumpers and skirts for me and jumpers and trousers for Peter, to be worn during the colder weather. 'Cast not a clout 'til May is out' was a well-observed maxim, so we wore our knitted vests and sheepskin liberty bodices until then, irrespective of unexpected heatwaves.

I particularly remember one occasion when we had both been made ready to go out and warned to keep clean whilst Grandma and Aunty Kalla got ready. Peter took it into his head to go into the farmyard; he slipped off the plank that covered the slurry and emerged covered in manure. His shantung suit and white shoes and socks were not recognisable!

My mother, during our period at the farm, was living and working in Maidstone but would come home usually every other weekend. She was always dressed very glamorously, changed her hairstyle (and colour) regularly, and, more importantly to my way of thinking, brought Peter and I a present! She and I shared a bedroom, and I remember how much I appreciated her presence. I was always very nervous of the dark, and it was comforting sharing my double bed. She had her own car—a grey Standard—and quite often, she would bring a friend home with her. That was how Monica and I were introduced because she, with her mother, came to visit. (Monica and her mother, Aunty Leah, were granddaughter and daughter of Mrs Gillam, the owner of the boarding house where my mother stayed in Maidstone.) My mother brought a breath of excitement to our daily routine; she was always very vivacious and talkative—entirely opposite to the down-to-earth personalities of Grandma and Aunty Kalla. And, wonder of wonders, she bought me clothes which were colourful and pretty. I particularly remember a turquoise coat and hat with yellow piping around the collar and hat and a turquoise and yellow bow on the crown of the hat.

On the first occasion when Monica visited, Peter and I were detailed off to show her the farm. Monica had not been on a farm before and was rather overawed by the animals. Peter tried to overcome that by pushing her into a pigsty with the pigs and closing the door on her. Her cries were heard, and she was rescued by not very impressed adults. She still remembers that incident.

My years at Park Farm were interspersed by breaks away. The first one of those was when I was about four; Aunty Kalla went to live at the vicarage to assist Mr Somerville, the vicar of Throwley, with his parish work, during the convalescence of his wife (Aunty Doris) from an operation for a brain tumour. Aunty Kalla had always been closely involved with the church—she played the organ for the services, was a bell-ringer, and took Sunday school classes. She took me to morning service, Sunday school in the afternoon, and then evening service, from an early age. I think that I went to live at the vicarage with Aunty Kalla to assist Grandma, and Peter stayed at the farm.

The vicarage itself was a very large house—wood panelled rooms, a study, a billiards room, beautiful grounds with two tennis courts, and stabling for horses. It was always very peaceful, in contrast to life on the farm when, even at night, the comforting noise of the horses in the stables, clumping their hooves on the brick floors, reverberated through to my bedroom. Everything in the vicarage seemed to happen quietly and efficiently. Of course, there was a housekeeper (Mrs Creamer). Meals were at a given time, served in the dining room at what seemed to me a vast dining table. I had to be called away from whatever activity I was involved in fifteen minutes prior to any meal to wash and 'do my hair' so that I was at the table before Mr Somerville came in and said grace before eating. Saturday was spent preparing for Sunday; no work was allowed on Sunday, so shoes had to be cleaned and clothes prepared. Breakfast was always a selection of cold food—ham, sausage rolls, etc., which I thoroughly enjoyed. However, I seem to remember that we had a full roast at dinner time.

I cannot remember how I occupied myself during my stay at the vicarage, other than that Aunty Kalla taught me to read and write so that when I went to school, I was well ahead of the rest of the class. I also learnt embroidery and presented Aunty Doris with a tray cloth that I had embroidered for her birthday. Looking back, it was quite an achievement for a four-year-old, and in later years, Aunty Doris reminded me of that. Prior to actually living at the vicarage, I had accompanied Aunty Kalla there for tennis parties—everyone dressed in white—followed by tea in the garden. Of course, the sun was shining, and it is a happy memory. However, my memories associated with staying there are of clouds of snowdrops on the banks of the drive in the spring and of white and deep mauve violets growing in a copse just along the road, which had the most lovely perfume.

Mr Somerville I cannot remember other than that he was a shadowy figure who was always there, but he had two elderly sisters who lived at the vicarage. They occupied a large bedroom on the side of the house and hardly, if ever, emerged from there; I think they were both in a pretty poor state of health. However, they did have two Pekinese dogs, who also lived in the bedroom, and I do remember the rather unpleasant odours that would catch up with one when passing the door. I also remember that it was a source of constant irritation to Aunty Doris. I was quite honoured on being allowed to walk one of the dogs, called Shenny, along the road for a short distance to enable her to eat grass and, when not walking her, being sent to gather suitable grass for the other dog; so my knowledge of dog medicine commenced at an early age!

I commenced school before I was five at Throwley. Aunty Kalla taught at the school at various stages, and she was very friendly with Mr and Mrs Harwood—Mr Harwood was the headmaster. They had a son, John, and he and I used to play together quite a lot. We went camping with the family and stayed on a farm near Hastings during a summer holiday. It was a hazardous business staying in a tent in those days since, if the tent was wet and you touched the side, a ladder would develop in the canvas! Additionally, the field would also be occupied by a herd of cows, who chewed up our facecloths that would be hanging out to dry on the ropes surrounding the tent.

Peter spent his early years at the farm without leaving it; Grandma once took him on holiday to Whitstable for a week, to stay with a friend, but had to return after three days because he cried incessantly. He hated leaving the farm. I think that that in some way explained why it was always me who went away, rather than him. My mother took me to Maidstone to stay with her at Mrs Gillam's boarding house, and Monica and I became good friends. I think it was between the ages of four to six and was for short periods only, but I did have quite a few weeks away when Grandma took me to Wolverhampton to stay with Aunty May and Uncle Jim (Yates).

Grandma had been suffering from gallstones for quite a long time, and she went to Wolverhampton for an operation. I think I am right in saying that she knew the doctors through her past experience as a nurse and that is why she went there. Aunty May was Grandma's youngest sister, who had two stepchildren from Uncle Jim's first marriage (Ena and Phil) and Joan from her marriage to Uncle Jim. He was the headmaster of a large school in Wolverhampton. They lived very comfortably at 44 Allen Road—a large semi-detached house. This was not a particularly happy period for me. Children were definitely seen but not heard! Aunty May was a strict disciplinarian, and when Grandma was not around, she was not really interested in my needs. Ena had quite a hard time of it. I cannot remember Phil, who was quite a bit older, but Joan received the most care and attention. Ena had to do a considerable amount of housework and had to wash up after each meal, and I was included in this regime. You had to eat everything that was put in front of you, and if you did not finish at one meal, it was put in front of you at the next meal and you had to finish it before going on. I remember one occasion when I sat at the table for ages being unable to cope with a cup of Horlicks. To this day, the smell of Horlicks makes me feel sick.

After lunch each day, we went to bed for an hour! I was not allowed to read in bed—I had to go to sleep. I suppose I was about six at the time and considered the whole thing rather babyish. Ena was my saving grace—she would take me out for walks to the local park and generally kept me amused.

Prior to Grandma going into hospital, we visited one of Grandma's other sisters, Aunty Min, who lived at the Knowle farm, Hixon, in

Staffordshire. Uncle Harry with his sons, Harry, Arthur, and John, lived there. Uncle Harry's wife, also one of Grandma's sisters, had been killed in a car accident, and Aunty Min had taken over the role of looking after the family thereafter. Uncle Jim had a car, and we went out quite regularly, visiting places of interest, so it was not all doom and gloom! However, the length of our stay in Wolverhampton was extended because of the need for Grandma to convalesce, and it was decided that I should attend school. In retrospect, I was quite a timid child, not used to the hustle and bustle of a big city and lots of people, and to be confronted by the size of the school to which Uncle Jim took me was quite unnerving. He took me to a class and introduced me to the teacher who, because I was related to the headmaster, gave me loads of attention and made me sit in the front. That did not help me to make friends with the other children, and it was quite a miserable time. At the end of the day, I had to go and wait for Uncle Jim in his office. On one occasion, a boy from my class had to report to the headmaster for some misdemeanour. I was waiting in the office for Uncle Jim and when this lad knocked at the door, which was half open, I hid behind it so that I would not be seen and peeped through the hinge crack, only to be confronted, to my consternation, by the eye of the boy on the other side! Not a word was said.

Grandma's convalescence took longer than anticipated, and Uncle Jim, Aunty May, Ena, and Joan returned me to Park Farm by car before Grandma's eventual return. That proved to be a fitting end to what had been quite an upsetting time; cushions were put in the well of the back seat of the car to enable me to lie down for the journey whilst Ena and Joan were wedged into the back seat with luggage, etc. I was violently sick about two hours into the journey and felt very unwell, and it was concluded that I had taken in exhaust fumes. I felt distinctly unwell for a few days afterwards.

It was a distinct relief to be back among my friends at Throwley School, back also to the daily routine of life at Park Farm. Grandma did not return until a week or two afterwards, and that was quite an event in itself. Grandad and Aunty Kalla went to meet her at Faversham (she had travelled home by train), and they were gone for longer than one would have anticipated, eventually arriving back loaded with parcels. They had been shopping and bought new eiderdowns and bedspreads for the bedrooms—gold for Grandma and Grandad's room, blue for the guest room, and pink for the room that I shared with my mother. That was followed by a visit from a lady who lived in Throwley Forstal, who spent quite some time decorating the upstairs—wallpapering and painting to great effect. The only room that did not receive attention was Aunty Kalla's, probably because she preferred simple white cotton throw-overs on the two single beds and plain colour-washed walls.

Grandad was rather an enigma; of course, he was kept busy with the farm, but our points of contact were not many. Some events do stand out: Haymaking, when an old open-top car was used to tow the rake and Peter and I were allowed to sit in the car during its slow progress up and down the field, turning the hay, and threshing time, when the wheat stored in the barn was fed into the threshing machine. As the bales were thrown down, they would dislodge the mice and rats who had made their homes there. Grandad, together with the farmhands, would stand on the floor of the barn and kill those rodents as they tried to escape. On one occasion, a rat managed to run up Grandad's trouser leg, and he thereafter resorted to wearing his boots and gaiters! He was a great lover of cats and, apart from the one indoor cat, there were at least twelve or thirteen wild cats with their offspring living in the farm buildings. Every day, after she had made the butter, Grandma would put a large pan of buttermilk outside the backdoor for the wild cats; it was a wide, shallow dish, and it was not unusual to see the whole rim occupied by cats and kittens, busily licking up the contents. Afternoon tea was always at five, and afterwards, Grandad would sit down in his armchair, having checked the time on the grandfather clock behind against his pocket watch and, if necessary, winding it up. At five minutes to six, the wireless would go on for the six o'clock news, and Peter and I had to sit quietly throughout its duration. Not a word was said, and woe betide anyone who made the slightest sound. I think that was where the saying 'little children should be seen but not heard' became most relevant.

During the long light evenings of summer, Grandad would quite often go for a walk down to the bottom of The Larches, and he was always accompanied by his cat. Once or twice a year, a local point-to-point meeting was held in fields opposite to the bottom of The Larches; a chain would be placed across the drive, and Grandad would sit there on a chair all day to stop people from parking their vehicles in front of the farm access. He was sustained in his vigil with food and drink prepared by Grandma and carried down by one of the farmhands. Occasionally, on Sunday evenings in the summer, Aunty Kalla would take Grandad, Grandma, Peter, and me on a visit to his old family home at Milsted, near Sittingbourne.

Every so often, Grandad would ask Aunty Kalla to stop the car, and he would get out, pull out a turnip from a field of another farm, cut a slice with his penknife, and eat it, checking whether the crop was as good as his! However, his health deteriorated greatly and, in the last eighteen months of our life at the farm, he was more or less confined to bed. One of the things I was able to do for him was go to the village shop and collect the *Kent Messenger* on Friday after school, for which I received 1d. Half of that I was allowed to spend on sweets, the other half had to be saved in my money box. And the sweets had to last for a week! The car—a singer—was comparatively new, and although I cannot remember that Grandad ever drove it, he was very proud of it. He would sit in the front seat alongside Aunty Kalla, wrapped in a blanket with his walking stick between his legs, greatly enjoying the change of scenery when we went out for drives. However, the singer did not like starting in cold weather, and 'horse power' gained a new meaning when one of the carthorses had to be used to tow us down the drive to get the engine going! That was a source of great annoyance to Grandad, particularly since my mother's car started easily in all weathers!

Latterly, Aunty Kalla took over the day-to-day running of the farm. I do remember that the cherries were sold on the trees, and the buyer was responsible for the picking, boxing, etc. The orchards were out of bounds to Peter and I—no longer were we able to go and help ourselves to fruit from the trees. During that period, one of the pigs farrowed and died, leaving thirteen piglets to be cared for. Aunty Kalla tried to hand-rear them, but all but one died. That one remaining piglet was an absolute character and followed Aunty Kalla everywhere, and if she was going out, she had to make sure that he was firmly locked up. However, on one occasion, he managed to escape and followed her to church, where he caused great amusement. She, at the time, was playing the organ. Since her name was Kathleen Mary, the nursery rhyme 'Mary had a little lamb' was changed to 'Mary had a little piglet'. He had a disconcerting habit of running his snout up and down one's legs and dirtying one's socks, which meant that Peter and I were always running away from him—usually with him in hot pursuit.

At about this time, I received a Christmas present of a fairy cycle, as it was called. It was a bike with hard tyres, and learning to ride it was a painful process, with many spills and subsequent scars on my knees to show for it. It did prove a trusty friend for many years afterwards, as I will recount. Both Peter and I did well at Christmas—we had pillowcases filled with loads of presents and woke very early on Christmas morning to find out what we had been given. A fire was lit in the front room, and all the meals on that day were eaten round the large dining table. This room also housed the Christmas tree and was decorated with paper chains that Peter and I had helped to make for weeks beforehand. Since my birthday was quite soon after Christmas, the decorations remained up for my party. The farmhands' children were invited for tea on that day, and we usually numbered about ten, tucking into the goodies prepared by Grandma. I well remember offering one of the children 'another cake' and being reprimanded for implying that they had already had one—an impolite thing to do! I was suitably chastened, and to this day I still wince when I hear that expression used.

Every year we went on Sunday school trips, once to Whipsnade Zoo but invariably to the seaside—usually Whitstable. There were also various parties held in the Village Hall for such events as Empire Day, but one particular event when we were shown lantern slides preyed on my mind for ages afterwards. That involved a bearded man lying in bed—obviously snoring although it was a silent film—and every time he opened his mouth a mouse popped in. He would close his mouth, and then the whole procedure would go on through again. I cannot remember how long that went on for, but the whole concept frightened me so much that when I went to bed I would dive under the bedclothes, not daring to expose my head in case the same thing happened to me.

A more happy occasion was when we were taken to see Walt Disney's *Snow White and the Seven Dwarfs* at the picture house in Faversham. I was absolutely enthralled with that. I was also taken to see Paul Robeson in 'Ol' Man River' and thoroughly appreciated the singing but got rather tired of having to sit still for so long.

I think it was during my sixth year that my mother came home to the farm to recuperate following a car accident. She had been sitting on the lap of Maurice Nealon in the front passenger seat of a sports car when the driver took a corner rather too fast; the passenger door flew open and my mother landed up in the road, sustaining severe grazing all down one side. She was encased in Elastoplast to cover the scars and spent a great deal of her time prior to returning to the doctor for a check-up, peeling off the plaster, bit by bit, to avoid the painful business of it being removed in one fell swoop.

In 1938, my mother married Maurice Nealon. I did not meet him until after the event; I do remember the occasion very well because I had to move into Aunty Kalla and Peter's bedroom. On the first morning of their stay, my mother, with her usual way out sense of humour, presented him with breakfast in bed—a dead mouse under the plate cover. He was not amused. I think I am right in saying that for the first year of their marriage they lived in a flat in Maidstone; my mother continued working as a hairdresser and Maurice with his employment, which I vaguely understood was in London. There was no formal acceptance by me, and I do not think by Peter either, that Maurice was 'Dad'.

Our life with Grandma, Grandad, and Aunty Kalla (Kaka) continued in its usual routine, except that Grandad was more and more confined to bed because of ill health. Also during that period, Mr Harwood, the headmaster of Throwley School, sustained a dreadful injury to his leg. He had told the children that the school field was out of bounds on that particular day because the grass was being cut, but a few children disregarded that instruction and chased after the tractor and mower. Mr Harwood, in trying to catch them, was himself badly injured. Aunty Kalla, who had helped out with teaching at the school from time to time, became a full-time teacher for quite a long period; I was in her class, which once again placed me in a somewhat awkward situation being seen by the other children as teacher's pet.

Uncle Ted (Cooper) was a frequent visitor to the farm. He had an old Austin Seven car, and I was always aware of his pending arrival from the distinct noise of its engine when he turned into the bottom of The Larches and chugged up the drive, trying to avoid the many potholes. He visited quite regularly when Mother first came home following her accident. However, it was Aunty Kalla who claimed his affections, and they were subsequently married in 1939. Uncle Ted came from quite a large family who lived at Rushmere; I knew one or two of his younger sisters who were at school with me—namely Ann and Norah, and I remember visiting the family home with Aunty Kalla from time to time. Neither Peter nor I attended the marriages of either our mother or Aunty Kalla, which, in retrospect, probably explains why both events did not really register with us. The final change in our lives at that time was moving from the farm, which happened before Aunty Kalla's marriage to Uncle Ted.

Throwley House, Harrietsham, Kent

I am a bit vague about the move. I think I went to stay with Aunty Bessie and her husband, Stanley Hooker, who farmed at Frinsted, near Sittingbourne. They had three sons, who would be my second cousins. My stay with them was of short duration only, and I eventually joined Grandma, Grandad, my mother, stepfather, and Peter at Harrietsham.

Throwley House was situated in the centre of Harrietsham. It was double fronted, but the roof at the back of the house sloped right down to the ground-floor ceiling level, which gave the two back bedrooms a very unusual shape. When you went in through the front door, you were faced by the stairs, with a door off to the left leading to a room that became Grandma and Grandad's living room. The door to the right led into a room that became the living room for the rest of us. A door at the back of that room went into the kitchen, and to the left of that was another room that had been a scullery. The whole house stood well back from the road, with a long frontage; there was a small-sized garden at the back, and, of course, the outside toilet was there.

A great deal of the best furniture from Park Farm came to Throwley House, which included all the 'front room' pieces—the sideboard with glass-fronted china case on top, the large dining table and chairs, Grandad's desk, the grandfather clock, and various occasional tables and chairs. A large oil painting and two glass cases of stuffed pheasants, which stood in the front hall of Park Farm, must have gone into the sale. On the large landing of the farmhouse, covering the complete long wall, there had been an immense cupboard with mirrors on the doors. Grandma and Grandad had had that built-in, and it accommodated all the household linen, etc. Because of its size, that too had to remain behind. Subsequently, the grandfather clock went to Aunty Kalla, and in its place, Grandma and Grandad gave Mum a mantelpiece chiming clock, which was also a wedding present to her and our stepfather.

Peter and I were enrolled at Harrietsham School. I made friends with the headmaster's daughter, Shirley Carter, who was my age, and used to spend quite a lot of time at her home. The family lived in the schoolhouse, next door to the school.

Grandad's health continued to deteriorate, and we were not allowed to play and make noise inside the house. He was latterly moved to a nursing home. Peter recalls that we used to be left in the car outside whilst Grandma and my mother visited him. Grandad passed away early in 1939—we had not been at Harrietsham very long. I cannot remember that impinging on me too heavily—in fact, I think like most things that went on we were kept out of the picture as we were considered too young to be told the full truth. I suppose a more charitable interpretation would be that we were shielded from the unpleasant and upsetting episodes.

Our stepfather's employment took him away from home a great deal, and we saw little of him. I always had the feeling that Peter and I were a bit of a trial to him; we had to tiptoe around in his presence. He would sit in his chair by the fire, reading his paper, but would rarely talk to us—I think children were beyond his ken, as the saying goes. He was a tall man, always well dressed, and, I seem to recollect, smoked cigars.

My mother converted the scullery at the back of the house into a hairdressing salon and operated a quite successful business. From as far back as I could remember, she had always done a haircutting round on her weekend visits to the farm, which included Grandad. And in my mind's eye, I can see him now, sitting on a chair outside the back door wrapped in a protective sheet, whilst Mum snipped off his curls (he had curly, black hair right up until the end). My haircut was not so welcome—my mother insisted on giving me an Eton crop, which was a fringe just above the ears on the sides and then tapered at the back, very much the same as a man's cut. I was never allowed to grow my hair long, a constant source of irritation!

On Saturday mornings, our living room was taken over by boys from a local remand home—waiting to have their hair cut. Mum also cut the hair of officers from the army camp, and I can remember two of them in particular who came to visit us socially during their time in Harrietsham. There was a singer called Hutch, who had a wireless programme. He sang and played the piano—and one of his songs was 'Yours' and another was 'I don't want to set the world on fire'. One of these officers had a voice very similar to Bing Crosby, and he would entertain us by singing these songs, among others.

We had two cats—one was a Manx cat called Tiger Tim. He adored my mother, and when she was sitting in her armchair, he would lie on the back of the chair with his head on hers and his front paws around her forehead. He also amused us greatly by running up the stairs at speed, through my mother's bedroom, down the two steps into my bedroom and jumping onto the mat on the linoleum floor—the whole impetus sliding him on the mat to the end of the bedroom. The mat had to be placed back in position to enable him to continue with his game or he would continue the same procedure in Peter's bedroom. What a character!

The first winter after our move to Harrietsham produced a very heavy snowfall, and in company with a large contingent of children from the village, we went tobogganing in fields just down the road from Throwley House. Peter and I would come in wet and frozen at dinner time, thaw out, change our clothes, and then go out for another session, until our mother put her foot down because we were running out of dry clothes. We then made a slide along the path leading to the back door and had great fun skating on that; unfortunately, that path also led to the outside toilet, and our stepfather put an end to our skating activities.

Both Peter and I were invited to a birthday party in Maidstone by our stepfather's sister; she had three children, and it promised to be a large affair. I was very excited at the prospect. I had a new party dress, which Mum had got made for me by a local dressmaker; it was pale blue satin, but the body of the dress was made with the dull side outwards and just the sash, buttons, and collar with the shiny side showing. Teamed with this were black patent leather ankle strap shoes—something that I had been angling for, for ages. Came the day and one of us—I cannot remember whether it was Peter or myself—was found to have a rash and temperature. German measles. No party and two very miserable children.

I suppose we lived at Harrietsham at that stage for about twenty months. War was declared in September 1939; it was a beautiful day, and Peter and I had gone the short distance to the station to meet a friend of my mother's off the train. Everywhere was peaceful, and then it was shattered by the siren going off. For the rest of the day, we were not allowed out of the house; quite what was expected to happen did not, but the apprehension of the adults filtered through to us. Grandma was on holiday in Aberystwyth with Aunty May and Aunty Min, and she immediately made arrangements to return home. She afterwards recounted how difficult it had been because the rail services were disrupted through troop movements, etc.

Aunty Kalla and Uncle Ted had been married the previous month. They bought a house in the village of Detling, not far from Maidstone. Uncle Ted was subsequently called up and went into the army. After the initial shock, life continued much as before, except that we were not allowed to roam too far away from the house. Blackout curtains had to be placed on all the windows, and the panes were criss-crossed with black sticky tape to lessen the risk of glass shattering should we be bombed. We were issued with gas masks, which we had to carry with us to school, where we had gas mask drill. The smell of the rubber of the masks was overpowering. I cannot remember how soon rationing was introduced, but I do remember that the local sweet shop curtailed the amount of sweets one could buy at a time—which in my case amounted to four gobstoppers for 1d, liquorice sticks, or sherbet. For a brief period, I found a way round this; my mother ordered the weekly provisions from a grocer's shop in the village, but during the week, when she ran out of anything, she would send me to the shop to collect the necessary item and put it on the bill. I made good use of that system for a short while by buying my sweets there and putting the amount on the bill also. It went on until the end of the month when the bill came in and I was rumbled, followed by a very severe telling-off and no pocket money.

Both Peter and I were aware, perhaps almost subconsciously, that Mum was pregnant. There was a lot of knitting-baby clothes—by both she and Grandma. The hairdressing continued, but I do recall how tired Mum would be by the end of the day and would sit with her feet up at every opportunity. When Maureen was born on 24 May 1940, I am not quite certain where I was—whether at Throwley House or away. But I do remember one evening shortly after her birth. Peter and I were both in bed, and Maureen was in her cot in Mum's bedroom; she and our stepfather had visitors. Maureen started to cry, and that went on for so long without any reaction from the adults downstairs that Peter and I both burst into tears, in my case inducing a nosebleed, and that combined to get the necessary attention, albeit a telling-off for us both for being so silly.

By that time, I was nine years old and had been put forward a year early to take the oral of the entrance examination to Grammar School, which I passed. However, when Maureen was about six weeks old, during the period when children were being evacuated out of Kent because of the air raids, it was decided that we would evacuate ourselves to Staffordshire, to the Knowle farm, Hixon, where Uncle Harry (Deakin) had offered us a safe haven. The subsequent move meant that I was unable to proceed with the written part of the entrance examination.

The Knowle, Hixon, Stowe-by-Chartley, Staffs

We travelled to Hixon by road. My mother drove the singer, and if my memory serves me right, we were followed by a smallish van which had all the luggage on board. The journey was made more difficult by the fact that the road signs had been taken down to confuse the enemy should they land; it not only confused the enemy, but it also confused Mum and our stepfather because we had great difficulty in getting off the ring road around London. However, get off we eventually did and arrived at the Knowle farm to a great welcome. I think Grandma had travelled independently and was already there. Maureen's father returned to Kent with the van the following day.

The Knowle farmhouse seemed vast in size to my child's eyes. It comprised four good-sized bedrooms, plus a room that was approached by a back staircase and was used as a storeroom for apples and pears—all neatly individually wrapped in newspaper to prevent them from going bad. Another two or three steps led out of that room to the bedroom used by Uncle Harry and the boys. The other bedrooms were served by the main staircase, which went up from the front hall. On the other side of that hall lay a large 'best room' (which had never been used since Aunty Jess's death) and a large living room, which housed a dining table, glass fronted bookcases, and various easy chairs around the fireplace. Coming in by the back door (the front door was never opened), the living room door was on the right, and a door on the left led into the dairy. Going down the passageway, the next door on the right led into the kitchen, and then, at the end of the passageway, was a storeroom and the door of the back staircase.

My mother, Peter, Maureen, and I were given a large bedroom at the end of the house, Aunty Min moved into a small bedroom to give Grandma her larger room, and Uncle Harry, Harry, Arthur, and John had single beds arranged like a dormitory in the large bedroom at the other end of the house.

And so we settled down to a routine that was not dissimilar to that of Park Farm. When we arrived, they were in the midst of harvesting, and on the first day, out in the fields having cadged a lift on top of a loaded cart, I jumped down to the ground, and Peter, following my example, did the same and fell and broke his arm. He had to be taken to the hospital to have it set; he says now that he did not feel any pain at the time. I had forgotten about that incident until he reminded me; what I do remember of our first few days there was how the stubble scratched my bare ankles and made them extremely sore.

I had always thought of Park Farm as 'large', but the Knowle farm would have accommodated two of the former. The milking herd alone numbered about sixty; there were fourteen carthorses and a few pigs. I cannot remember that there were sheep, and latterly, the pigs went. It was mainly arable and dairy farming. John, the youngest of Uncle Harry's boys, was just finishing his school life at Rugeley Grammar School and then joined his brothers and father working on the farm. They all got up very early for milking, and when that was finished, they went into the large kitchen for an immense cooked breakfast prepared by Aunty Min. Then they were back to the routine tasks of mucking out the cowsheds and feeding and grooming the horses, to name but a few.

For the first few weeks of our stay, it was school summer holidays, so Peter and I tagged along in whatever activity was taking place. He was still having to cope with his arm in a sling. Grandma and Mum helped out with the cooking and cleaning, and of course, Maureen was still very young and needed quite a lot of attention. The Knowle farm was very isolated—Hixon village being about one and a half miles away, and because of petrol rationing, the car was not used very often. However, that was where my fairy cycle came into its own; I would go off to the village on that to get items from the shop for my mother. Uncle Harry became very attached to Maureen; he would take her out in her pram for walks, and as she got older, he would carry her around to places that were inaccessible to the pram.

School time came around; Aunty Min arranged for us to go to Stowe-by-Chartley School. She was a great friend of the schoolmaster and his wife, Mr and Mrs Prince, so to Stowe-by-Chartley Peter and I went. Peter started school about two weeks after me because of his broken arm. It was about two and a half miles from the farm and we used the fairy cycle; I would stand on the pedals and pedal, and Peter would sit on the saddle. We had frequent spills, but it did tend to make the journey to and from school a bit quicker. On the way home, dependent on the whereabouts of the cows, for whom we both had a healthy respect, we would cut across the fields into the back of the farm, but if the cows were grazing there, we would go the long route, up the main drive into the farm. A herd of about sixty or seventy cows running around with their tails in the air can be a rather daunting sight, and Peter and I, on the way home from school one afternoon, sheltered in a fenced-off waterhole to escape their attention. This self-same waterhole was the home of quite a few moorhens, and Aunty Min would cook moorhen eggs and chips for our tea, so it was a popular 'port of call', in any case. We both got a lot of ribbing from the boys about our fear of the cows. I think my concerns stemmed from an incident that had taken place at Park Farm when Grandad had been sitting outside the farmyard gate, keeping an eye on a cow, which was due to calve. She had a habit of trying to escape from the farmyard when she was due, and to prevent that, a wattle gate had been placed on top of the main farm gate to stop her jumping over it. However, she took a slightly easier route and jumped over the adjacent wall and over me (I was playing next to the wall) into the garden. Grandad thought I had been killed, and there was such a commotion; Grandma and Aunty Kalla came rushing out of the house; that memory stayed with me throughout my childhood.

In retrospect, I can appreciate what a wonderful person Aunty Min was. She worked so hard in so many different areas of farm life that it is hard to understand how she coped. Grandma did the bulk of the cooking while we were there, and Mum helped in the house and outside on the farm. But that did not cover so many tasks undertaken by Aunty Min. Monday was washing day when the copper was lit and all the 'whites' were boiled, starched, and, dependent on the weather, hung out to dry or over the very large clothes rack in the kitchen. She did all the dairy work, which involved carrying the milk from the cowsheds during milking (with a yoke on her shoulders, balancing two pails of milk) and feeding the milk into the cooler and then into the churns. This was a procedure followed after milking both morning and afternoon. Then, of course, the equipment had to be sterilised and the dairy swabbed out, followed by wet mopping of both the kitchen and passageway floors.

Peter and I were banned from going into the house until the floors dried, which was not too bad in the summer but not appreciated in the winter. A keen gardener, Aunty Min had a large lawn surrounded by flower beds in the front of the house, and behind that, a very extensive kitchen garden where she grew all the vegetables for everyday use plus fruit bushes—blackcurrants, redcurrants, and, hitherto unknown to me, white currant plus gooseberries, raspberries, and strawberries. I am talking about a very large area, but there was rarely a weed to be seen, and the flower borders were an absolute picture in the spring and summer. She lifted all the bulbs once the tops died down and dried them out in the sun ready for replanting in the autumn. The fruit was bottled and jammed as it became available, and Peter and I helped with the picking; there was one particular dessert gooseberry for which I developed a strong liking, and a lot of them found their way into my mouth!

Peter and I were given our own plots to cultivate; they were on either side of the path leading to the outside toilet. We were given nasturtium, marigold, Love-in-a-mist, and Californian poppy seeds, and our patches were a riot of colour in the summer and gave us both a lot of pleasure. A task that was not enjoyed so much was weeding between the bricks of the path, which led to the toilet!

Aunty Min also made a lot of wine—mainly elderflower and elderberry but also plum and damson. It was known as 'cheer', and a spot of 'cheer' was taken every day by Grandma, Mum, and Aunty Min—for medicinal purposes, of course! And, my goodness, it was potent stuff. Mum and Aunty Min got on 'like a house on fire', and the pair of them would quite often disappear into the pantry/storeroom, where the 'cheer' was stored, emerging somewhat later, both with red faces, and giggling like a pair of schoolgirls. On one occasion, there was a loud explosion from the pantry, and it was subsequently discovered that two large demijohns of wine had 'blown' their contents all over the place.

Aunty Min also looked after the chickens, which produced the eggs for the family's needs. It was a time of food rationing, and farmers were limited in the amount of milk they could hold back for their own consumption; it meant that the amount of cream available for butter making was only that off the top of the household supply of milk. Aunty Min, ever resourceful, would save as much cream as possible over two days, and because it was not sufficient to use the butter churn, she would put it in a glass sweet jar with lid on and rock it backwards and forward on her knee whilst sitting in front of the fire in the evening. The small amount of butter that it produced hardly seemed worth the effort. She would use the remaining buttermilk to wash her face in, and she always had the most perfect, wrinkle-free, skin.

My mother and grandmother were always knitting—Aunty Min rocking the sweet jar backwards and forward!

Another memory of Aunty Min is connected to the carthorses. One of the mares died after foaling, and Aunty Min hand-reared the filly, which was quite a difficult thing to do. She was named Blossom. When we arrived at the farm, Blossom was about a third grown and did not appreciate that she could no longer go charging up to Aunty Min in the field for attention—she knocked her twice to the ground. So Aunty Min had to stand behind the gate and make a fuss of her. However, when she was full grown, Blossom had to be 'broken in', and the breakers had to spend three days at that—running her round and round on a rope. It seemed so cruel, and Aunty Min was very upset to see Blossom put through such agonies. All to no avail, since she never became a good working horse in a team.

In the first few months of our stay at the Knowle farm, Mum and Aunty Min would go off to Rugeley Market once a week by car. However, petrol rationing began to bite, and then Aunty Kalla came to take the car back to Kent—a prior arrangement agreed between her and my mother. So Mum and Aunty Min resorted to biking backwards and forward to Rugeley. On one of these trips, they had been laughing so much about something or other, and Aunty Min's false teeth dropped out of her mouth onto the road and broke! That was the cause of even greater hilarity when they got home and told the tale!

When Maureen was about six months old, she had a chest infection and ran a high temperature. This brought on a convulsion. Very luckily, Grandma was on hand, and she plunged Maureen alternately into cold water and then into warm water to bring her around. It was an extremely frightening episode, but thank goodness, Maureen suffered no after-effects. Shortly after that, Peter and I both went down with measles. Peter suffered from running a very high temperature because it left him with a slight heart murmur. We were both confined to bed in the large bedroom that we shared with Mum and Maureen, and as we began to get better, we began to get bored with nothing to do. In the event, we started to make models out of matchboxes and used matchsticks—I remember making a pram and matchstick dolls. I cannot remember what else we made, but I do recall Uncle Harry popping in to see how we were getting on and also he being highly intrigued at our endeavours. Getting a constant supply of empty matchboxes was more of a problem, and we used matches from my mother and the boys who conveniently all smoked.

When we were once again mobile, I made a trip to the village shop on the fairy cycle. The shopkeeper was talking to a lady when I arrived, and as she droned on and on, I could feel everything going black and I felt dreadfully sick. I stood by the counter for what seemed like ages, trying to prevent myself falling down, and eventually everything returned to normal. I did not tell anyone about that, but a few days later, the shopkeeper told Grandma that I had 'gone as white as a sheet' and that she had been very worried about me. I wish she had helped me at the time! Grandma surmised that it had been too much effort required in cycling to the shop so soon after recovering from measles.

I think we had two Christmases at the Knowle farm, but neither stand out in my memory; I cannot even remember whether there was a Christmas tree, although I am sure there must have been. I can recall the extremely heavy snowfall during the second winter of our stay, when the snow was so deep and frozen that the hedges were covered and the farm animals were able to walk from field to field without impediment. The milk lorry was unable to get through to collect the milk churns left at the bottom of the drive every day. And I was very concerned about the farm dog, who was chained to his kennel in the wall of the bull shed. He and I had become friends from the outset, and I used to take him for walks down the fields—the cow less fields! Otherwise, his task was to repel invaders to the farmyard.

Stowe-by-Chartley school was not very big—I suppose it was a typical village school, rather like Throwley. I had made friends with a girl called Jean Astle, who lived about halfway on the route to school, and Peter and I would play with her and her brother when possible, although they attended Hixon school. Mr Prince introduced gardening lessons twice a week, and if the weather was fine, it would quite often be three or four times a week that we were out digging, hoeing, and planting vegetables for the war effort. Luckily, I was left with a love for gardening, which has remained with me ever since.

I was reminding Peter about the concerts we used to give to the family, but he could not remember these occasions. That involved making use of the grain loft above the cowsheds. The stage was an area cut off from the seating by empty sacks hung over the low beams as curtains. The seating comprised full sacks of grain arranged in a row, and there the family audience, plus Edwin, the farmhand, had to sit and endure our recitations and singing! Edwin would grumble about having to rearrange the sacks of grain; Uncle Harry thoroughly appreciated our efforts.

Picking up on what I gleaned from the adults about Uncle Harry, I had always understood that he was still grieving for Aunty Jess. The dreadful part of the accident in which she died was that Young Harry had been driving the car. I gathered that that had affected Uncle Harry's relationship with Young Harry—which would be understandable. I do think that having children around him during our stay helped him considerably. He adored Maureen and, in his quiet way, would share jokes with Peter and I. During the mushroom season, he would get us out of bed very early in the morning to go mushrooming, walking through the fields heavy with dew and looking for them. Then we would go back for a breakfast of eggs, bacon, and mushrooms. He also taught us how to gather watercress from the streams that abounded in the lower fields—never to pick from stagnant water and always from moving, clear water. We used to go with him quite often to get the cows in for milking, and he would point out how they would always walk in a single file. On one such occasion, he drew our attention to a badger at the foot of a tree in the wood we were passing—the only time I have seen one in its proper setting.

There was only one other farm worker, apart from the family, working on the farm. His name was Edwin—a man of few words. He chewed tobacco, and it was not safe to go near him when he was milking because he would spit his tobacco saliva to the farthest distance possible from the cow. I found this completely incomprehensible—how could anyone enjoy chewing tobacco?

I suppose John would have been about sixteen when we went to the farm, Arthur about three years older, and Harry three years older. They were close brothers and worked well together; Mum would join Arthur and Harry in many of the farm and social activities, particularly when they visited neighbours on adjoining farms. She used to go riding occasionally with the wife of the adjacent farmer, and I was invited to ride a pony belonging to one of their children. This proved rather disastrous. Once I was made to sit on the back of the pony without a saddle. The farmer gave its rump a slap and it took off with me into the middle of a pond, where it stood and started to drink; not having a saddle to hold on to, I started to slide slowly over its head. Luckily, it stopped drinking at the vital moment and lifted its head, thus enabling me to hang on for dear life. This episode put me off the idea of riding thereafter.

During the period of our stay at the Knowle farm, Maureen's father visited once for about three days. I understood that he was engaged on 'essential duties', which involved the secret service, without really knowing what that meant. The war impinged on us very little apart from us being aware of food rationing and sweet rationing, the latter more obviously affecting me! There was one occasion when, together with the adults, we observed a glow in the sky for about three nights running from the bombing of Coventry. Aunty Min had warned Peter and I not to accept lifts from strangers to and from school; walking home one afternoon, feeling hot and tired, a car stopped alongside me and the driver offered me a lift, which I accepted. However, once in the car, I remembered Aunty Min's words, panicked, and asked the gentleman to stop and let me out, which, thank goodness, he did. I later learnt from Aunty Min (of course) that the 'gentleman' was a local farmer, and he had recounted that episode, at my expense, with great hilarity.

We had occasional visitors to the farm—Aunty May, Uncle Jim, and Joan from Wolverhampton and members of the Cunningham family from Liverpool (one of Grandma's sisters—Aunty Flo—married a Cunningham, who had a fruiterer's business in Aintree). Grandma occasionally went from the farm to stay with the other members of the family, who had all emanated from Stone, in Staffordshire. The family name was Thompson.

I think we had been at the Knowle farm for about seventeen months when Grandma returned to Harrietsham. At the time, the reason given for this was that two incendiary bombs were dropped in the front garden of Throwley House, which, luckily, had not exploded and which had been removed. However, Grandma wanted to make sure that the house was not damaged in any way. I subsequently learnt that she had received a letter from Mr Firminger (the gentleman from whom Throwley House was leased), in which he implied that our stepfather was bringing other ladies back to the house. Grandma found evidence of that on her return and she was very upset at the general state of the place—it was, after all, her home, as well as ours.

So we were once again on the move, back to Harrietsham, leaving behind at the farm a very sad Uncle Harry and Aunty Min. They had been so kind and caring to us during our stay, and it was hard to imagine what awaited us on our return to Kent.

During subsequent years, Grandma often went to Wolverhampton and then on to the Knowle farm for a visit, and on returning on one occasion, she gave us the sad news that Blossom had got caught in the bog of a waterhole. Although she had been pulled out, the strain had been too much and she died. In addition to that, the farm dog, who had been my great pal during our stay, pined away and died following our departure. Aunty Min was convinced Blossom died of a broken heart; I think it also applied to my doggie friend.

Return to Throwley House, Harrietsham

I cannot recall the return journey. I have a vague feeling that it was by train—Mum, Maureen, Peter, and myself—but no detail remains with me. When we got back to Throwley House, we saw evidence of the incendiary bombs that had fallen in the front garden—a large crater. I was very aware of the strained relationship between Mum and our stepfather, and he did not spend much time at home.

I returned to Harrietsham School and almost immediately had to sit the eleven-plus exam. This involved going to Maidstone Grammar School and joining other children in a large hall, where we sat at individual desks and complied with verbal instructions to complete the papers that were handed out. I was completely overawed and apprehensive and found it impossible to concentrate. It was not surprising, therefore, to subsequently learn that I had failed.

We had not been back very long before I gleaned that we were on the move again. I remember snippets of conversation between my mother and Grandma about moving arrangements and, more particularly, Grandma saying to Mum that she would come with us and 'look after the children' on the understanding that there would be no more men 'on the scene'. I think it is true to say that the war going on above our heads in the form of air raids, forewarned by the sirens going off, almost took second place because of the burden of knowing that we were leaving Harrietsham—and leaving our stepfather.

In great secrecy, a removal van appeared one morning and loaded up our furniture and belongings. The arrangements had been made to coincide with our stepfather's absence 'on duty'. We had seen so little of him before going to Hixon, and certainly since our return, that I can remember feeling quite a sense of relief that we were going to make a new start without him. Grandma would be there for us, as she had always been.

Hill Mount, Charing

Hill Mount was a delight. Situated at the top of Charing Hill, it commanded a glorious view of Charing and the surrounding countryside. Mum had leased it from a family called Vance. Most of their furniture was stored in the third bedroom, and we had the use of two bedrooms, a large lounge with a bay window that encompassed the abovementioned view, and a kitchen with a Rayburn that heated the water for the bathroom. To have a bathroom was luxury indeed! Whilst it had electricity, Throwley House did not have a bathroom, and both Park Farm and the Knowle farm had neither electricity nor a bathroom. And here we were, with both! The whole property was surrounded by a large lawned garden with a few morello cherry trees.

My mother had established a hairdressing business in Charing village a month or two prior to the move. It was in the front room of a house in the centre of the main street; the rest of the house had been leased to a Mrs Hyatt, who had moved down from Scotland with her son to be near her husband who was in the army and stationed nearby. She and my mother became good friends.

A routine was quickly established. Peter and I attended Charing School, and we would walk down the hill to the village with Mum in the mornings whilst Grandma would stay at home and look after Maureen. During the weekends, Grandma would go over to Detling to stay with Aunty Kalla, returning on Sunday evenings to look after us. I can remember enjoying the normality of life during the first few weeks; we attended Sunday school on Sunday afternoons, something which had been missing from our lives since leaving Park Farm. At that stage, perhaps the only blight on the landscape was the fact that our next-door neighbours owned two dachshunds, and on our return from school in the afternoon, they would dash out of the garden, bark, and snap at us. So eventually we wised up to that and did not cross over the road until we were beyond the gate to their garden.

Insidiously, things began to change. Mum would go to the Wagon and Horses on Saturday evenings and eventually would be brought back by Bert. To begin with, he just dropped her off but then started to stay the night, which stretched into the weekend. He had a car and was living with his sister Dolly at Challock. At that time, he was driving lorries for Greens who provided pit props to the coal mines upcountry. This usually meant that he was away for most of the week, but eventually his stays with us became longer, and Grandma was very unhappy about the situation. I had to move out of my mother's bedroom and for a short while shared with Grandma, and Peter had a camp bed in the lounge.

And then the three of us came down with scarlet fever. I think Peter was the first to go to the Isolation Hospital near Ashford, followed by Maureen and then me. Certainly, his stay did not overlap with mine, but I was there for most of the six weeks with Maureen but not in the same ward as she. I did not feel particularly ill during that time but was immensely bored with the lack of activity. I would help the nurses make the beds and look after the younger ones. Since they did not wish to upset Maureen, my mother and grandmother did not visit us, so on visiting days, when the other children's parents arrived to peer through the viewing windows at their incarcerated offspring, Maureen and I felt quite deprived.

We did get a visit from a lady who lived with her mother halfway down Charing Hill. I had made friends with her on my walks home from school; she and her mother had the most lovely garden, and she had invited me in to see it and subsequently given me tea. I do not know whether that friendship emanated from my mother, but however it happened, she very kindly visited me in hospital and brought some 'fake' marshmallow (squares of jelly dusted with icing sugar). I was absolutely delighted with that but not so impressed when Sister took possession of it so that it could be shared out with all the other goodies that had been brought in for the other children. Maureen went home about ten days before me, and I had a short visit from my mother then.

At some stage on our return, Peter and I acquired pet rabbits. I think we had about three or four of them. They had hutches along the wall outside the back door of Hill Mount. My own rabbit was a large black male, who was called Bogey; he was quite vicious and would bite and scratch, given the chance. Peter and I put together rabbit runs with wood and wire mesh, and during warm weather, we would put these 'runs' on the lawn with the rabbits inside to give them an opportunity to nibble on the grass. We became expert at looking for rabbit food in the hedgerows and acquiring plenty of dry grass for their hutches, which we cleaned regularly. Bogey took every opportunity to escape, and we were forever running to catch and return him to his hutch.

During the school holidays, Peter and I amused ourselves by 'playing houses'. Under the shade of the trees between Hill Mount and next door (the owners of the dachshunds), where the grass did not grow, we planned the layouts of downstairs and upstairs of the house, delineating the boundaries/walls with lines of soil swept up from the middle of the 'rooms'. This produced quite a bit of dust; Peter and I used to get well covered in that, but it did not diminish our enjoyment of the game. However, the next-door neighbours complained bitterly to Mum about the quantities of dust invading their house from our house making, so our game had to stop.

The gardens of Hill Mount were mostly lawned, and whilst it was possible to keep some of the lawns under control with the mower, there were parts of it that grew too long to be mowed. I once set to it with a billhook, and on one swipe through the grass caught a grass snake, cutting it in half. We subsequently saw a further two or three of those snakes, so further forays into the long grass were curtailed.

We were aware of the war mainly because of the long convoys of troop-laden lorries and equipment, which would wend their way up Charing Hill to the vast, camouflaged army camps in the woods about a mile farther on. There would be the occasional air raid and heavy gunfire, and at night the searchlights would scan the skies. There were stringent blackout precautions, and because of its prominent position at the top of the hill, together with the size of the windows, Hill Mount was quite a difficult place to make safe. Street lights were not allowed, and on one occasion, in Charing village, walking home in the dark with my mother, I turned to say something to her and walked straight into a lamp post—nearly knocking myself out in the process.

Grandma had become increasingly unhappy about the situation vis-à-vis Bert, and things finally came to a head when Peter badly scalded his foot; he had got up early in the morning and was trying to make a cup of tea, and he managed to spill boiling water over his ankle and foot. As we removed his sock, the skin came away with it. Grandma, coming back from Detling to be confronted with this, said she could no longer cope with the situation and departed back to Detling, taking Peter with her. This meant that there was no one to look after Maureen during the day, so my mother advertised for a housekeeper. To begin with, Mrs Hyatt at the salon would look after Maureen while my mother was hairdressing, but we eventually had a housekeeper. She was a small, prim, single lady, who one could imagine would have been well suited to the 'upstairs, downstairs' type of domestic service but seemed to find children bewildering, particularly a small, active child like Maureen. She occupied what had been Grandma's bedroom, and this was when I went into the camp bed in the lounge. And, as Grandma had done, she departed at the weekends.

Bert, by that time, had virtually moved in. Prior to Peter's departure with Grandma, his influence over us had begun. On Sunday afternoons, instead of going to Sunday school, Peter and I were sent off to the woods on the opposite side of the road to gather firewood for lighting the fire during the week. I think this one act alone alienated us both; we had both been brought up to regard Sunday as a day of rest, when you wore your best clothes and kept clean and tidy, and here we were being sent off like ragamuffins to gather firewood while Mum and Bert went for a rest. We had to take Maureen with us in her pram, and on one particular Sunday afternoon, Peter and I decided to walk to Throwley. We had not been back there since our departure from the farm, and I think, to both of us, Throwley represented a way of life that was fast slipping away—values that did not apply to our day-to-day existence with Mum and Bert.

Since Grandma's departure, we were not loved and cared for. We walked and walked to Throwley Forstal, past The Larches to Park Farm, and on to the church and vicarage. This was some considerable distance from Charing Hill, and by that time, we were both tired and hungry and Maureen was getting fretful. I remembered that one of my teachers from Throwley School lived adjacent to the church, and I knocked at her door. Luckily, she was in with her husband; I think she was quite upset to see us in such a state, and she invited us in and gave us something to eat and drink. She insisted on contacting Mum by phone via the owner of a garage up the road from Hill Mount. We then had the return walk home with Maureen in her pram, and when we did finally arrive, it was to find that Mum was not very pleased with us.

The first housekeeper did not last for long; she objected to Bert's presence, having to cope with the additional cooking and cleaning when she had originally been taken on to care for Maureen. We then had a second housekeeper, a big, buxom lady, who did not remain with us for long either.

Maureen reminded me that that lady had a drink problem, and once when she was under the influence, Maureen got hold of a bottle of sherry and consumed quite a large amount; luckily, she did not suffer any ill-effects. She was subjected to so many changes whilst still virtually a baby.

My mother and Bert would dress up on Saturday evenings and go off to the Wagon and Horses, leaving me on my own in the house to look after Maureen. I was very nervous of being left (Peter was at Detling at the time), and as it would grow dark, I would sit in the bay window with the blackout curtains drawn behind me, willing my mother to return. The searchlights would be playing across the skies during raids, and I would be so frightened that Maureen would wake up and cry since it meant traversing the dark hall to get to her bedroom. On one of those occasions, there was a terrific banging at the back door. I was petrified and burst into tears when eventually Mum and Bert returned. We never did find out what had caused the noise. My reward for being in charge on these evenings was a bag of crisps and a Vimto!

Following the departure of the second housekeeper, Maureen was left each morning with a childminder, who lived in a house at the entrance to Charing village, and collected on the way home in the evening. At lunchtime, I would leave school and join my mother at a cafe at the bottom of the village for a cooked meal, which meant that she did not have to cook in the evening. Sunday was the only full day spent at Hill Mount when we had a cooked dinner.

When we first moved to Charing, Mum paid for me to have piano lessons from a lady in the village, but I did not persevere with the necessary practice, so those were discontinued. Also, when walking home after a lesson one dark evening, I was convinced I was being followed. Every time I quickened my step, the footstep behind me quickened its pace. I kept glancing behind me but could not see anybody, and by then thoroughly scared, I started to run up the hill. And then I discovered, to my intense relief, that the 'footstep' I could hear was none other than the buckle of my coat belt, which was hitting the ground each time I took a step. Any thoughts I may have had about continuing with lessons were finally laid to rest after that episode. However, I got great pleasure in strumming out a tune with one hand on the piano in the lounge, and it was an enjoyable pastime on cold winter evenings.

Thinking of Charing School does not evoke any particular memories. I suppose I was not long there since the scarlet fever isolation of at least six weeks took out quite a large slice of time. I must have been about eleven when we moved to Charing, and we lived there for about a year. I cannot recall having any friends other than the daughter of our next door but one neighbour. She was called Vanda, and she and her mother had moved out from London to avoid the bombing. Both mother and daughter were always immaculately dressed. Vanda was a great source of envy to me because she had long, blonde hair, worn in ringlets, whereas mine was still very short and straight. And somehow their perfection emphasized my drabness.

Our lifestyle was not a very happy one, and we had no contact with the rest of the family at that stage since Grandma and Peter were with Aunty Kalla and I particularly missed them all. Added to that was the knowledge that my mother was now heavily pregnant and not married to the person with whom we were living—that in itself was quite a difficult situation for me to accept. I did not like Bert—he was already getting 'heavy' in various ways. I thoroughly appreciated the facility of bathing daily, but he stopped it on what was probably an excellent premise—that the Rayburn used too much coke to heat the water. But the fact that it was he and not my mother who made that decision was hard to tolerate. I think the final straw was when, having consumed rabbit pie for Sunday dinner, I was told by both of them that I had just eaten Bogey, my rabbit, who had been missing for sometime. I had searched high and low for him for about ten days, going up into the field at the back of the house. Mum thought that it was a huge joke, and both she and Bert were highly amused at my indignant and hurt response when they told me what had happened.

At about that time, my mother discovered that the childminder who had been looking after Maureen had not been treating her very well—confining her to her chair for most of the day rather than letting her move around and play. Moreover, I think, there had been a problem over the little amount of food she would be fed. I cannot remember the exact details, but Maureen then went to Grandma and Aunty Kalla at Detling.

My mother and Bert took me with them to look at a house in Ashford, where they were thinking of moving. And that was what eventually happened; Mum sold the salon and with the proceeds bought 236 Hythe Road, Ashford. So once again we were on the move—with all Grandma's furniture—to a new home.

Reflections—One

I have to try and put things into perspective before I proceed with the narrative of events. To start with, both Peter and I had been brought up in a stable, loving, and caring home (Park Farm), where Grandma and Aunty Kaka provided us with the parameters of acceptable behaviour. Prior to her marriage to Grandad, Grandma had been head nursery nurse to one or two titled families and her maxim was never to smack or raise the voice when dealing with bad behaviour but to speak quietly and firmly to the offending child. It certainly worked. She would produce a 'saying' to reinforce her point when dealing with a problem.

'A rolling stone gathers no moss.'
'A stitch in time saves nine.'
'Early to bed, early to rise, makes a man healthy, wealthy, and wise'.
'The early bird catches the worm.'
'Cast not a clout 'til May is out.'
'Little children should be seen but not heard.'
'Red sky at night, shepherd's delight, red sky in the morning, shepherd's warning.'
'Time and tide waiteth for no man.'
'Cleanliness is next to godliness.'

And there many more, which I am sure I will remember from time to time. She also had a fund of nursery rhymes plus a rhyme that she used on young children to get them to sleep. Holding the child's hand she would go from finger to finger, singing the following song.

'Dance thumbikin dance
Dance merrymen all

Thumbikin he can dance alone
Dance a merrymen everyone.'

Together, she and Aunty Kaka provided us with a home life that never questioned the absence of our father. I can never remember, in the Park Farm years, of being aware of the absence of our father; he was not talked about, and I suppose it had something to do with the fact that neither was our mother there on a daily basis. She flitted in and out of our lives every other weekend so that when she married Maureen's father (I was about eight) it did not affect our daily routine until we moved to Harrietsham. Here our mother looked after us because Grandma was heavily involved in looking after Grandad, who was very ill. We now, of course, had a stepfather, but he did not spend much time at home because of a demanding job, so our acknowledgement of him as 'Dad' was not really defined. He was a male figure who did not really impinge on our daily life, and, of course, Grandma was always there in the background.

With the outbreak of war and the Battle of Britain, our subsequent move to the Knowle farm once again placed us in a father-less position—not that it made any difference to us. But I am trying to put across the fact how, when we moved from Charing to Ashford, it was to an entirely different home regime, where we did not have the loving care of Grandma.

It has to be said that with the advent of Bert at Hill Mount, everything changed. Grandma departed to Detling, followed by Peter. The two housekeepers departed, mainly because of disagreements with him, and the whole tenor of life changed. Our mother was heavily pregnant and not married to the father, which was a source of great embarrassment because nice people did not behave like this, and I did not like feeling ashamed of my mother.

The other factor that had been affected by so many changes was our schooling. I had not felt at a disadvantage with lessons until I started attending Charing School. I seemed to have missed out in various subjects but particularly in maths, which dented my confidence because I had previously been quite competent in that subject. I had, of course, missed six weeks during the scarlet fever isolation. I hated changing schools with the consequent need for forming new friendships, so the thought of breaking into a new school setting bothered me greatly.

I hope this explanation goes some way in explaining my state of mind when we moved to Ashford.

236 Hythe Road, Willesborough, Ashford, Kent

When I had first visited 236 with my mother and Bert, I had been favourably impressed. It was the third one of three identical properties in a terrace, and 236 was adjoined by a further row of houses of a different type; the immediate property adjoining 236 (left facing) was a hairdressing salon. The house at 236 comprised a basement (which was virtually ground floor at the front but a definite basement at the back), ground floor (again with the distinction of being approached by steps at the front but ground level at back), first floor, and attic. The reason for the different ground levels between front and back was explained by the fact that when the excavations for the railway line running along the end of the immediate terrace were made, the resulting soil/earth was spread over the area where the three houses were subsequently built. That raised the level quite appreciably between the front and back and also between the next terrace's back gardens. There was a small front garden and quite a long back garden with an alleyway at the end. This brought one out on the side of the railway embankment, where there were allotments that belonged to the three houses—one each, and then out onto Hythe Road just before the railway bridge.

The basement at the front was approached by three steps down and then into a small porch, which was, in fact, the underneath of the steps leading up to the front door. There was a coal house under the lower part of the steps—opposite the door to the house, which opened onto a hallway. From there, on the right was a door to the front basement room. Straight ahead was a staircase; to the right of that were two more doors, one leading into what had been used as a second coal house, and then lastly the kitchen, which contained a copper, an old type of glazed sink, and a kitchen range. The window looked out onto a sloping-outward stonewall with iron railings at the top. The staircase led up to the ground floor, where, turning left, was the toilet and a lean-to wooden shed, and then out to the garden. On turning right at the top of the stairs, the layout mirrored the layout of the basement with two rooms, front and back, the hallway with the front door, and the stairs leading up to the first floor. The first floor had two rooms, a boxroom, and a further staircase leading up to a room with windows front and back, which spanned the whole house area. The three rooms on the front of the house had bay windows with the exception of the attic. There was no bathroom. All the main living rooms and bedrooms had fireplaces.

Although the property had not been lived in for a year or two—like a number of houses, it had probably been vacated when the previous occupants had moved away to a safer area during the Battle of Britain—it was comparatively warm and dry. To begin with, Peter and I shared the attic bedroom, divided by a makeshift screen, with Peter sleeping on one of the iron single beds that had been in Aunty Kalla's bedroom at Park Farm. Maureen and I shared a double bed in the back part of the attic. The front room on the first floor was Grandma's bedroom, and the bedroom behind it was used by Mum and Bert. The ground floor front room was Grandma's sitting room. The basement front room became the family living room, and the kitchen behind it—dark and unwelcoming—became the hub of the house. I mention how 236 was initially 'laid out' because in the ensuing years it was reshaped/revamped a great deal.

I think we all looked forward with optimism to a new start. Taking on board the restrictions imposed by the war—rationing, blackout, air raids etc.—at least we anticipated being together again as a family. Grandma returned shortly after we had settled in, bringing Maureen with her. Maureen reminded me of that; she was dressed in a red coat and hat, looking absolutely lovely, and was so excited that she went up the steps to the next door instead of 236!

And so Peter and I commenced at our new schools; he, at ten years old, started at Willesborough School, whereas I, then thirteen, went to the North Central School. What a revelation it turned out to be—a large, airy, modern building with a separate site for the boys on the other side of the playing fields. I was placed in the top class for my year, and although I did not have long at the North, I certainly gained tremendously academically and in confidence during that period. I made some good friends and in particular one (Mev), and we remained close for the rest of our school days. Of course, we still had to comply with certain restrictions imposed because of the war. We had to carry our gas masks with us at all times, be ready to evacuate to the air raid shelters when given the necessary instructions, and if the air raid sirens went off, not to venture out of the building until the 'All Clear' sounded. The large windows of the classrooms were criss-crossed with sticky tape to prevent them from shattering in the case of bomb blasts, but although there had been a few attempts by the Germans to bomb the railway works in Ashford, luckily, the school was not affected.

We wore uniform—navy skirts, V-necked pullovers with white blouses, and a navy and yellow striped tie. The day started with 'marking the register' in our classroom, our names being called out by our form teacher, and then filing down the stairs to the hall for assembly. Afterwards, we dispersed to the designated classroom in accordance with our timetable. A new item to my list of previously unknown subjects was domestic science and there was also a science lab., but for some reason or other I did not take it; I think it was an either/or situation, and girls were routed towards domestic science! The food-rationing situation limited the scope of what could be undertaken because the ingredients for the dish to be cooked had to be brought from home. I cannot remember taking home anything of particular outstanding culinary achievement at the end of the day!

A further enjoyable subject was PE, which included exercises in the assembly hall on the bars and other equipment and hockey outside on the playing fields when the weather was good enough.

Another welcome addition to school life was dinner in the school canteen. The canteen was used by both sites, and although situated at the entrance to the girls' site, the sittings were staggered to allow the boys to have their dinners either before or after the girls. In the main, it was good, wholesome food, and I cannot recall being unable to eat anything because of 'likes and dislikes'. We were also supplied with a bottle of milk at the first 'break' of the day at around eleven in the morning.

School life was good, but the same could not be said of home life. Bert's job was graded as a compulsory occupation, which meant that he was not eligible for service in the Forces. He certainly worked hard for long hours in all weathers and, to begin with, spent days away from home driving supplies of pit props up north for Greens, the company for whom he worked. I think money was short at that time because my mother was no longer in business and heavily pregnant, and he had acquired a ready-made family of three children, a fact which he regularly pointed out to us in language that did not leave anything to the imagination. This was the man who we had to call 'Dad'. A saving grace for me with the move to

Ashford was the fact that nobody would know that Mum and Bert were not married, but the downside was that I had to call him Dad, and that I found very hard to do.

During that early period at 236, I had the flu, and to this day I can remember how ill I was; every part of me ached, and I ran such a high temperature that I was delirious, which caused my mother to get up in the night and tend me. I had been moved downstairs into the 'front room' on the ground floor and was sleeping on the camp bed—again! It really took its toll, and when I did eventually get up and go downstairs to the kitchen, my mother was in the middle of a washing session, which involved the heavy use of bleach to whiten the 'whites'. The smell of the bleach made me feel quite sick so back upstairs I went.

Barclay arrived on 23 May 1944 and was born in the back room on the ground floor, which was being used by Mum and Bert as their bedroom at that time. His arrival almost coincided with the advent of the doodlebugs—the Germans' rocket-propelled missiles. Those were, in the main, aimed at London, and to begin with, efforts were made to shoot them down. This caused more problems because they were unpredictable, and although intercepted over the coast, they would quite often come down before reaching London and other vulnerable areas. Then RAF planes tried to bravely send them back from whence they had come, turning them round by tilting the wings, which was a very tricky and dangerous manoeuvre. They made a distinctive noise, heavier than that of planes, and when the engine cut out, there was an eerie silence before the explosion, which meant that it had come down. In the front room of the basement, we had a Morrison shelter—most people were supplied with one to protect them from falling masonry should their house be hit by a bomb. The shelter was a large table, made of steel, with a base that could be used as a bed.

I mention this because the doodlebugs (V1s) did not give people much chance to get to a shelter. During the bombing raids, when the siren went off, people automatically went to a shelter and remained there until the 'All Clear', and a lot of people slept in their shelters. Our next-door neighbours had an Anderson shelter in the garden in which they slept every night. I mention this background to illustrate how Barclay arrived during a time of great stress. The nights and days were disturbed by the noise of frequent raids, and we needed to be constantly vigilant. The practice in those days was to put your baby outside in its pram to sleep in the fresh air, but it was a hazardous thing to do. I think that everyone was at a pretty low ebb health wise at that time and particularly my mother, who had never been a domesticated person and who found coping with a new baby hard going.

It is hard to believe now, but coping without a bathroom was second nature then. There was a flush toilet by the back door on the ground floor, but bath night involved getting out the large tin bath housed in the unused storeroom/coal house next to the kitchen in the basement. The water was boiled in the copper and baled out into the bath. Subsequent emptying was also by hand into the kitchen sink. It was quite a comedown after the luxury of a bathroom in Hill Mount.

During this period, Grandma spent most of her time with Aunty Kalla at Detling, and some time after Barclay's birth, following a disagreement with Bert over the way in which he treated Peter, Maureen, and I, she left and did not return for many years.

It was at about this time, or at least when Barclay was about three months old, that arrangements were made by the authorities to evacuate all children of school age away from Kent because of the continuing threat from the V1s and then V2s. At about the same time, my mother was informed that I had passed the admission exam for the newly created Technical College in Ashford. In the event, Peter and I were evacuated to Torquay. We were separated because we went in groups according to the school we attended. I ended up in Babbacombe, and he was on the other side of Torquay. However, I was lucky enough to be placed next door to my friend, Mev. There were two other evacuees from London in my billet, and we three shared the large front bedroom. They were much younger than me, and the only time I saw them was usually at night! Our landlady provided us with good meals (it was here that I was introduced to tripe and onions, which I thoroughly enjoyed but which I have never had since) and looked after our physical needs, but one never felt 'at home'. It was a different story for Mev, next door; her landlady was a lovely person, and she would include me into various activities, which she organised for Mev's benefit.

Our education was provided at a Technical College in Torquay, where I can honestly say I did not learn a thing. I am a bit vague on dates, but I think we arrived there at the beginning of the summer holidays so we had this spare time before college started the autumn term. We had to be assimilated into groups of older students, who were already a year ahead of us, and it was quite a shambles. Moreover, we had lectures and free periods, and the free periods greatly outweighed the lectures.

The big compensation was being in such a lovely place with freedom to go to the beaches. We received pocket money weekly from our landlady, as did all the evacuees, and Grandma would send a postal order with her weekly letters. Mev and I went to visit Peter on one occasion, to find him happy and settled in his 'billet'.

My mother had gone to Wendover to stay with Bert's parents, taking both Maureen and Barclay. Bert's father was a gamekeeper on an estate there. By all accounts, he was a bad-tempered man, and although I did not experience it, Maureen, then four years, did.

We remained in Torquay for about four months. Mev went home earlier—her parents came to collect her. Peter and I, with the rest of the evacuees, returned home by train with our cases and gas masks. The whole period had left me in limbo—cut off and not touching-down with the familiar things of life, particularly attending school.

My mother had returned from Wendover with Barclay and Maureen quite a bit sooner than our return from Torquay. She and Bert had moved the kitchen from the back room of the basement to the back room of the ground floor and had installed a black kitchen range in the fireplace and a sink and gas cooker in the adjacent corner. Certainly, it was an easier arrangement for access to the garden rather than having to go up and down the narrow and dark stairs to the basement. Bert had planted up the garden with vegetables, and at that time, there was a large apple tree—Cox's apples, I think—towards the end of the garden.

I had the impression that Peter's and my return was not particularly welcome, and I suppose the reality was that Mum and Bert had enjoyed their time alone without us. Barclay, at about six to seven months, required a lot of care and attention. He was not a happy baby—cried a lot—and it is not difficult to understand why he was like that when one considers the stress Mum was under before he was born and then the noise and explosions caused by the V1s and V2s. Before we were evacuated, a V1 was brought down in the field of the Grammar School, which was farther down Hythe Road on the opposite side to 236. I was making my way down to the basement when the resulting blast blew me down the last few steps. Barclay was only a few weeks old at the time.

Peter returned to the North Central, and I started my schooling at Ashford Technical College. The uniform was navy V-neck pullovers, navy skirts, white shirt, and navy ties with a cross stripe in green and red. Because a few of us had missed the beginning of term, we had quite a bit of catching up to do in subjects that were completely new to us—shorthand, typing, book-keeping, French. But we had some marvellous teachers: Ms Ringrose for the first three subjects, Ms Calvert for French, and then a lovely lady, Ms Allchin, for English and speech training. We had a headmistress, Ms Coward, and principal, Mr Pincher. Mev and I were firm friends among a group of girls who were great characters—Jean Spicer, Peggy Bean, Molly, and one or two others whose names I cannot remember. The only subject in which I lost out because of having missed the first few weeks of term was French.

Life at 236 was pretty grim. Bert's behaviour towards Peter, Maureen, and me exposed him for the bully he was. He would rant and rave about our supposed misdemeanours, and the sound of him coming down the garden path in his heavy boots at the end of the day raised my stress levels considerably. He had imposed a regime of jobs for us to carry out. The day would commence with his standing at the bottom of the attic stairs at six thirty and bellowing for us to get up (with embellishments). It was Peter's job to blacklead the kitchen range and then light the fire. This was followed by cleaning shoes and getting the coal in for the day. I had to cook his breakfast (the table was always laid the night before), and then out to the front door I went to clean the brasses. Then it was back to the kitchen to wash up and have our somewhat meagre breakfast before taking my mother a cup of tea, and she would then get up with Barclay. I then had to make the beds before getting ready for school.

Biking to school, up East Hill, I would often wonder how my life would have been if I had taken up Grandma's offer to send me to Ashford High School for Girls as a boarder. I was later given to understand that my father had offered to fund that. It was a fee-paying private school and on my way to the Tech. I would pass 'snakes' of girls in their smart grey and red uniforms, making their way from the residences to the main site. Somehow, it reflected the way of life I might have expected as compared to life at 236, but it was first mooted when we moved from Charing when I was anticipating a normal home life!

Home in the afternoon, having had a school dinner, I would go straight upstairs to change out of my school uniform and then down to the kitchen to get tea. Mum always made a cooked dinner at lunchtime, and Bert's was served on a plate and reheated in the evening over a pan of hot water. Maureen, Peter, and I had our school dinners, so it was bread and margarine tea for us. As soon as Bert would get in and had his dinner, it was washing-up time—with warm water from the kettle. He would watch what I was doing, and if he considered I had taken too much warm water he would start to bad-mouth me. Trying to wash up in greasy water with the water getting dirtier and dirtier was no mean feat. I continually suffered from cracked and chapped hands.

Mum and Bert would sit on either side of the fireplace, which was surrounded by a high fireguard usually covered in drying clothes, and I would sit at the table doing my homework. Seeing me doing my homework was like a red rag to a bull; I was conscious of his rage building up, which did not help my powers of concentration on my work. Usually, in any case, Barclay would start crying upstairs, so I was immediately detailed off to go and rock him to sleep. It would often take at least an hour before I could quietly creep out. Then Bert's sandwiches had to be cut and prepared for his lunch the following day. He always took two flasks of strong black tea with him, and those were filled in the morning.

The weekends were organised for us; Saturday morning washing was done by hand in the sink in the basement. My mother coped with the nappies and baby clothes on a daily basis, but I did the washing for the rest of the family. Because of the nature of his work, Bert's clothes were always very difficult to get clean and involved quite a bit of scrubbing of collars, etc., and the use of the inevitable bleach to get his singlets clean. Then I would go upstairs to clean the bedrooms after changing the sheets. I had always been an avid reader. From Park Farm days, I had been very content to sit down with a book. And the 'cleaning the bedroom' exercise gave me an opportunity to spend a few quiet moments catching up with whatever book I had on the go—usually one of the rather lurid paperbacks that my mother had delivered with the paper on a weekly basis. I would get carried away time wise with the resulting telling-off.

Recounting all that, I am amazed at how much Bert found it necessary to control us. I was always very conscious of being clean and tidy, and my first upset with him had been at Charing when he had stopped me from having a daily bath. Now it had extended to how often we changed our clothes for the wash. I wore white blouses for Tech. and was only allowed to wear two a week. Inevitably, the collars, after two days of wear, looked dirty particularly since my hair was quite long, but woe betide me if he saw more than two blouses on the line at the end of the week. I would try and get round that by surreptitiously washing just the collar and drying it ready for the next day.

My mother was at a pretty low ebb at that time, and she did say that had it not been for her commitments in relation to the house and Barclay, she would have 'taken off' again. Although much of Bert's nastiness was directed towards us three children, the constant shouting and swearing obviously had an effect on her, but she felt powerless to do anything to protect us. Quite often, she would say things, which would make him worse towards us, and to give her the benefit of the doubt, she was in such a nervous state that I think it was unwittingly done. Later on, I think it was a learned pattern.

Of course, times were hard. The air raids had receded, but food rationing, the blackout, and petrol rationing were still in force. Bert had to do one night a week on duty as a fire-watcher in the belfry of Ashford church. My mother was always very frightened of being left alone on those nights. We did keep a few chickens in a chicken run at the end of the garden, and those produced a few eggs to supplement the egg ration. This was supplied in dried-egg form, which was very useful for cake making and particularly nice when scrambled on toast. The butter ration was very small and supplemented by margarine. Bert had the butter ration on his sandwiches. Dried milk was another supplement, although in a household with young children there was an allocation of fresh milk. Mum always had the cream off the top of the milk in her tea—probably an offspin from Park Farm days.

On one occasion, Bert was offered a piece of pork by a friend who was killing a pig. This had to be done with great secrecy because it would have been seen as 'black market'. However, Peter, Maureen, and myself in the back of Bert's recently acquired 'old banger', my mother with Barclay on her knee in the front alongside Bert who was driving, off we went into the country to collect the said pork. We were invited into the house of these people for a cup of tea and given the joint of pork that landed up on my knee for the return journey, which had to be before dark because the lights on the car were not reliable. In cranking up the engine to get the car started, smoke and flames burst out from the bonnet. We three in the back piled out of the car with great haste, and the prized joint of pork rolled into the road! The fire, caused by oil from the sump dripping down into a tray underneath it, was duly put out; we all got back into the car and with some trepidation proceeded home.

Clothes rationing was something we had all got used to. People were very resourceful in making things from old items; sheets when they wore out in the centre were remade middle to outside, and everything was patched or darned. For our first Christmas in 236, I knitted slippers for Grandma's present and padded the cardboard soles. She, in turn, unravelled old woollies and remade the wool into jumpers or cardigans, after first having stretched the wool around a piece of wood to get rid of the crinkles from the previous knit. Another clever innovation was making a rag rug. All available pieces of material were cut into strips of one size and then woven into a piece of coarse sacking. When the whole of the sacking was covered, the back was lined with whatever was at hand—as long as it was heavy enough. In the fireside rug in the kitchen, one could identify various bits of clothing from us all! There was a wartime saying, 'Make do and Mend', which was something most people resorted to in various ingenious ways. I particularly remember that in *Women's Weekly*, a very popular magazine, there were always good tips on how to make the most of one's rations, with recipes for producing tasty dishes with unusual and non-rationed ingredients, and patterns for making over/cutting down and combining the good parts of worn out clothing. I think that was where I got the knitting pattern for Grandma's slippers.

At about that time, Bert's sister, Aunty Dolly, came to live with us. She had left her husband and was heavily pregnant. She had the first floor front bedroom, previously Grandma's, and this was where her son, David, was born on 29 January 1945. Bert's behaviour towards us carried on as usual—constant vilification and, in Maureen's case, physical punishment. It became so bad that, for once, my mother did intercede; he would hit Maureen around the head and she had earache, and it was later discovered that she had a pierced eardrum. Whether this was a result of his heavy-handedness I cannot say, but it certainly contributed to the earache from which she used to suffer. Before David was born, Aunty Dolly would help with Barclay and Maureen and take them out in the afternoon for a walk.

Part of the early evening ritual in that first winter was to fill the water bottles and put them into the respective beds. Had Bert had his way we would not have had such a luxury because it meant using hot water heated on the kitchen range. Peter and I had stone bottles, which were very effective but which had to be well wrapped up and covered because woe betide you if your foot came into contact with an uncovered part of the bottle in bed. We were instructed to put the water bottles out of the bed once we were warm, but invariably I would be asleep before that happened. Once the bottle fell out onto the bedroom floor and broke. Since my mother and Bert slept in the bedroom underneath mine, it did not go unnoticed! I eventually received a tin hot-water bottle, which, although it did not break, did get quite dented from falls from the bed! Another bone of contention was the window in my bedroom. Once when the doodlebug came down in the Grammar School playing field, the blast blew out the glass from that window, and for some considerable time, it remained covered in boarding. When it was eventually repaired, I was delighted to have an opening, a see-through window again, and I would open it by securing it on the latch. However, one night the wind got up, lifted it off the latch, and blew it back with such force that the glass broke. So it was not just the water bottle but also the broken glass that became the topic of my misdemeanours at every available opportunity.

It must have been in the spring of 1945 that Mum encouraged Bert to go into business on his own by buying up tracts of woodland, felling and selling mainly as pit props for the coal mines. He took a lot of persuading, and, of course, it required quite a capital outlay to get started. I can recall that he went to auctions of woodland, having first surveyed the appropriateness of the timber on site. At about the same time, my mother had also managed to rent the orchard at the back of 236 and one of the lock-up garages, and that was where the car and lorry were kept at night. Since Bert had a petrol ration for the business, it augmented the sparse ration allowed for the car. Not that the car was used very often; my mother was very apprehensive about driving it since if driven over 30 mph the front wheels developed the jitters, which I understood was caused by the need for new brushes. The only way to stop that problem was by stopping and starting again, so the progress of any journey was slowed down considerably.

I do not think that Aunty Dolly stayed with us too long after David's arrival. When she did move on, it was to live with her parents in Wendover but left quite a few of her belongings behind at 236, and those were stored in the boxroom on the first floor.

Barclay's early progress was marred by constant chest colds; he was not a happy baby, and there was always this constant need to rock him off to sleep, whether in his pram or in his cot. Mum's health was at a pretty low ebb at that time, and the doctor suggested that she drink a milk stout daily to build her up. She faithfully obeyed! At regular intervals, either Peter or myself was despatched to the local pub's (The Fox) off-licence—usually at lunchtime—to return the empties and get a fresh supply of both cigarettes (she had always smoked Craven A) and stout. I think this was the beginning of her later problems with drink.

In the early days of the business, money was a bit tight, and we had a lodger, a gentleman who was a proofreader for one of the local papers. He was a dedicated bachelor in his early fifties and had little in the way of conversational skills. The first floor front bedroom was his, together with the front room on the ground floor. Without a bathroom, he used the washstand in the bedroom, and a large jug of hot water had to be left outside the bedroom door for his ablutions in the morning. Both his breakfast and dinner were eaten at the table in the kitchen, and he would then depart on his bike to work.

It was my job to clean his bedroom weekly, and on one of those occasions, I noticed that he had left the top drawer of the chest of drawers open. I spotted a bag of chocolate biscuits. To my shame, I could not resist taking one of these and on a further two or three occasions not just one but two biscuits. He in turn discovered that his chocolate biscuits were disappearing and told my mother, who gave me a 'right telling-off'. I felt intensely guilty about that incident for ages, and although my contact with that gentleman was not much, I was very relieved when he moved on, which coincided with the basement being let to Frances and Bill. Frances was a sister of Aunty Kalla's husband, Uncle Ted. They did some work on the old coal house adjacent to the then kitchen and turned that area under the stairs into the kitchen and the old kitchen into a bedroom. Apart from the toilet, they were then self-contained, having their own front entrance.

Following the invasion in June 1944, the war had been taken to the enemy, and by the time peace was declared on 8 May 1945, we had become used to life without the constant need to be vigilant about the possibility of air raids, etc. VE day was celebrated by hundreds of people dancing and singing in the middle of Ashford, as happened in every city, and then subsequently street parties were organised although that did not happen in our neighbourhood. I was not allowed to go up to Ashford to join in the initial celebrations. One of the most notable things was—*no blackout*. It was absolutely amazing to see people's house lights shining forth as though every place had suddenly burst into life. Of course, the war in Japan was still carrying on, but that did not pose a threat to our safety in the UK.

I was really enjoying my schooling at the Technical College, but the restrictions imposed at home made it hard going. Everything came before my need to complete homework in the evenings. Bert really resented the fact that I was not earning my living—at that time the school leaving age was fourteen. During the school holidays, I had to join him fruit picking and on one occasion ended up at Park Farm cherry picking. I thought my feet were going to break in half after a day of standing on the struts of the ladder in inappropriate footwear, which did not support my feet. However, at the end of the season, I had earned enough money to give some to my mother and then to buy myself a new bike—a utility model, all black—which served me well for many a year. I always biked to the Tech., and at the end of the school day, I would occasionally go home with Mev, who lived in South Ashford—not stopping but just for the company. It was a longer route and meant that I did not get home as quickly.

Bert, coming home early one evening and finding that I was not there and getting the tea, put a stop to that. It is hard to understand why he felt the need to be so controlling. My mother told me one day that our next-door neighbour, Aunty Gladys, had remarked that I always looked unhappy—had changed from the early days of our arrival. I am sure both she and her mother could hear Bert's constant verbal abuse. My mother could not understand that. Maureen would quite often escape over the fence between us and next door to go and see Aunty Gladys, who would make a fuss of her, but she in turn got into trouble for that. I remember going to Tech. one day after a particularly vicious verbal going-over from Bert and breaking down to Mev. She told the headmistress, Ms Coward, who interviewed me, but when she put before me the action that could be taken by the authorities I could not face that and assured her that I was really all right.

I know that Peter and Maureen were going through their own unhappy times, but we were all so wrapped up in our own particular problems that it made us oblivious of each other's concerns. Whilst I do not wish to give the impression that every day was a 'bad' day, it was the constant apprehension of what Bert's mood would be like when he came in from work in the evening that wore one down. We used to wryly say that he was worse at the time of the full moon, and that did have some validity. When his business got going to the extent of employing someone (I think his name was Eddie), I understood that he came in for the same treatment.

During the school summer holidays in 1945, I was allowed to spend a week with Aunty Kalla at Detling. At that time, Bert had a motorbike, and Detling was en route to the place where he was working, so he would drop me off—literally, as it happened—because my legs would be so frozen that when I got off the pillion I would fall to the ground. Thank goodness, the return journey was by bus.

It was a week of sheer bliss to be with Aunty Kalla. How two sisters could be so entirely different is hard to understand; Aunty Kalla was so loving and caring, and the atmosphere in the home was always happy. She was an excellent manager, and although Ian was still very young, she still provided Peter, Maureen, and myself with a refuge. In fact, Peter and

Maureen had lengthy stays and attended school in Detling. Grandma remained with Aunty Kalla as well, but she had itchy feet, as they say, and was always taking off to her sisters in either Wolverhampton, Hixon, or Liverpool. Uncle Ted was still in the army. To return to 236 at the end of the week was not something I looked forward to.

Our form mistress at the Tech. was Ms Allchin. She also took us for English, and this encompassed elocution lessons. We were taught how to breathe properly from the bottom of the stomach and throw our voices—to be heard at the other end of the room. As an additional aid to further these skills, she really caught our imaginations by involving us in a puppet show production of *Treasure Island*. We had to produce hand puppets, first making a clay model of the face and then covering with a papier mâché mask. When this dried out, it was removed from the model and the mask was filled with padding, forming the back of the head. A neck was inserted to allow for a finger to hold the head in position when the puppet was being played. I think the hair was provided by wool sewn into the back of the head, and then the puppets were clothed in items appropriate to their role, allowing a finger to be inserted in both sleeves. A few of us (including Mev and myself) had been busy writing the book of *Treasure Island* into a play. Ms Allchin had managed to cajole a carpenter friend into making a puppet theatre, and after quite a few practice sessions, the puppet play was performed for the whole of the school. Although I had made a puppet, I was selected as compère. It was such an ingenious way of educating us into the power of speech.

Bert's reaction to my homework of making a puppet was incredulous, which meant that I had to contrive to hide it away as much as possible.

Saturdays were always taken up by household tasks, and Bert worked a full day. Sunday, when he was at home usually all day, did not differ much in our routine except that my mother cooked a Sunday dinner for which we all sat around the table in the kitchen. Mum and Bert then retired for a rest, and Peter and I would wash up, and if the weather allowed, take Barclay out for a walk in his pram. By this stage, my mother had developed a few baking skills which involved fruitcake, so at teatime, the table was laid with bread and butter, jam, and fruitcake. It was a most uncomfortable meal because Bert would watch how many pieces of bread and butter I took and how much jam I took. In today's parlance—where was he coming from?

In 1946, following a miserable Christmas, we acquired a dog—Dusky—who was a great pet. It would have been difficult to identify her antecedents, but she was black with brown and white markings and was about the size of a Border Collie. To begin with, she was not allowed into the house, but she slept in the lean-to shed by the back door. This shed was used as a dumping ground for Bert's tools, heavy boots, and rainwear. In the early days at 236, we had acquired a cat, which produced kittens in the shed. It must have been during hot weather because both the cat and the kittens were flea-ridden, and I, with my obsession for cleanliness, used some antiseptic powder to dust the kittens to kill the fleas. The dreadful thing was that the mother cat licked the kittens to clean them, and it was poisoned by this powder. The kittens had to be put to sleep. I suffered agonies of guilt over this—an action taken in good faith to kill the fleas resulting in such a painful end for the cat.

On my way to and from Tech., I biked past the boys' grammar school that was just on the other side of the railway bridge from 236. I quite often ran the gauntlet of being whistled at and would carry on with a rather red face, trying to ignore their attention. However, on one occasion, I was stopped on the way home by a boy, who handed me an envelope. This contained a poem which said how beautiful I was and how he would like to meet me. I am not doing justice to his words because it was really a lovely poem. I did try to respond, but my efforts were pretty poor, and that was the first and the last time that I received such poetic admiration!

It was at about this time that, following a school medical, the doctor found that I had a slight curvature of the spine. I had to attend the clinic weekly and do exercises, which I was supposed to carry on with at home on a daily basis. I did not suffer any discomfort from this condition.

Towards the middle of 1946, it was obvious that my mother was again pregnant. The cessation of all hostilities—the war with Japan was celebrated by V-J Day on 12 September 1945, following the dropping of an atomic bomb on Hiroshima by the Americans—she was in a much happier frame of mind, planning for the new baby. One of her big wishes was to get a high pram—a coach-built model—rather than the utility models, which had been available throughout the war years. Barclay's pram had been a second-hand pram because that was all that was available at the time. The knitting needles began to produce baby clothes in white wool—white was the accepted colour for new babies. The layette also included long clothes, which consisted of flannelette undergown that was worn under a long-sleeved fine cotton, long-sleeved, embroidered gown. My mother had saved those used for Maureen, followed by Barclay, and now they were to be used by the new baby. I think this is where the term swaddling came from—being wrapped up as warmly as possible.

Bert and my mother now occupied the front bedroom on the first floor, and I had to move down to the back bedroom with Barclay for the inevitable rocking sessions to get him off to sleep. When Christopher was born on Christmas Eve in 1946, Barclay was about eighteen months old. I had to miss Tech. to look after Barclay and cook the meals a week or two prior to Chris's birth, and I was quite upset about this because I had been involved in a play for Christmas. Christmas Day was spent looking after the family.

When the new term started, it was hard going with shorthand and typewriting speed tests to attain RSA certificates. One lighter and more enjoyable subject was the forming of a music club by the then principal, Mr Pincher. To begin with, it was sessions with gramophone records of classical music, interspersed with him playing the piano, which he did with great brilliance. The once-weekly meetings of the music club were held after school, and because of this, I had to fight hard to be allowed to attend, but these musical sessions opened up a new world for me and really awakened an appreciation of the classics, particularly violin and piano concertos.

My recollections of the ensuing months prior to leaving the Tech. at the end of the summer term do not evoke any special memories. Of course, there was even more to do on the domestic front. My main memory is Bert's strong opposition to my continuing for another year at the Tech., which I would have liked to have done to gain my School Certificate. However, on Ms Coward's recommendation, I was sent to the North County Modern Girls' School to be interviewed for the position of school secretary and was offered this job at the princely salary of about £18 per month! I finished at the Tech. at the end of the summer term in 1947, having passed RSA 60 wpm shorthand and Intermediate typewriting exams and started at the North at the beginning of the autumn term.

It was a strange feeling, returning to the North as an employee! The Headmistress Ms Butler was new to me, but this did not help to overcome my feelings of still being a pupil as a few of the teachers had taught me during my brief time there. However, I had a very pleasant office opposite to the headmistress's office. The job was not particularly onerous, and I settled in quite quickly. I attended evening classes at the Tech. to further my speeds in shorthand and typewriting, and whilst I did miss the company of my good friend Mev and a few others, the new regime took over and occupied my time.

My standing in the home did not alter, but at least it could not be thrown at me by Bert that he had to keep me, which was one of his favourite topics! I had to give my mother the greater part of my salary at the end of each month, but at least I was left with sufficient in my pocket to give me a sense of independence. I would walk home to midday dinner and then return to work. The routine in the morning and evening remained much the same, but there was a slight variation at the weekends. On Saturday afternoons, I had to do the shopping for my mother, usually walking to Ashford with Chris in his pram. Having acquired the coach-built pram for him, I cannot remember that Mum ever took him out for a walk, and a chance remark by someone that 'Hadn't I got a lovely baby' was quickly explained as 'He is my brother'. I was two weeks off sixteen when Chris was born, and it would have been a genuine misunderstanding. No one could deny that Chris was a lovely baby—a contented, happy child, who benefited from the overall improved living conditions, which prevailed after the end of the war. Rationing continued for quite some time, but items were becoming more plentiful in the shops.

At work, I had quite a bit of contact with the secretary on the boy's site, and we became good friends. She was engaged to a local lad and saving hard to get a home, so our contact was confined to work. During school holidays, we both had to carry on with a daily routine in an empty building. The teaching staff disappeared at the end of term and reappeared at the beginning of the next term, and I would be quite lonely. The caretaker opened up in the morning and closed up in the evening so the only people around were the grounds staff. Quite often, having nothing to do, I would go over to her office for a chat, or she would come over to see me. One of her brothers was a groundsman, and he would occasionally join us for a cup of tea. He invited me to go to the pictures, and I accepted. We duly met up one evening, me in my new camel coat on which I had sprayed some recently acquired perfume. I enjoyed the film, but I did not enjoy his company. When he asked me to go out with him again, I declined with the excuse that my parents would not allow this. This did not deter him as he called at 236 and spoke to my mother, asking whether she would give permission for me to accompany him to the pictures! Thank goodness, my mother said that I was too young to have a boyfriend. For once things worked in my favour! However, my perfumed coat, although new, was not worn for quite some time, because the smell of the perfume made me feel sick.

Once a week, I would go to evening classes, and the only other freedom was on Sunday afternoons when Peter and I were allowed out on our bikes, having first washed up after dinner. We had to be back in time to lay the table for tea, but we would get quite a way in the time at our disposal. The route usually followed the same pattern—out to Wye through Kennington and then back along the top road, which brought us into the top of Willesborough. When the weather was nice, we thoroughly enjoyed these sorties.

From our early days at 236, Mum had paid into the Pearl Assurance Co. a small amount every week in the individual names of Maureen, Peter, and myself. This was collected weekly by a representative. I think our respective policies had been started by Grandma—probably at Harrietsham. As I was the eldest, my policy matured first. Mum pocketed the proceeds as she subsequently did with both Peter's and Maureen's proceeds. It obviously did not bother her that Grandma had intended that these monies would help us in our early teens. In fact, Mum did not ask us for permission, and it was purely by accident that I found out about it some time afterwards.

Even though I was working, my social life was non-existent, but I did persuade Mum to come to the pictures with me to see Nelson Eddy and Jeanette MacDonald in a film entitled, as I recall, *Maytime*. We had to come out halfway through because she was worried about having left the children with Bert. Always a very nervous person, Mum had become more so during the war years and found it hard to relax other than in the home environment.

I was aware that Mum's divorce from Maureen's father could not go through until they had been separated for three years, and this finally happened in about mid-1947. There then had to be a period—three months I think—before it was made absolute. Before Mum and Bert got married in Ashford Registrar's Office on 14 February 1948, Mum had asked both Peter and me whether we would change our surname from Heyman to Raines by deed poll. We both said 'No' for obvious reasons but also because Heyman had quite a significance in that we had learnt over the years that our great-grandfather was titled Sir Peter Heyman. During his lifetime, he had created a scholarship for any boy named Peter Heyman to attend Kings' School in Canterbury. Although this had not been invoked for Peter, there was still this sense of pride that our great-grandfather was a 'somebody'. Maureen was subsequently adopted by Bert, and she became Raines from Nealon. Also, around this time, there was a notice in the local paper asking about two children with the name Heyman. I remember some discussion between my mother and grandma about this and their decision not to take any action. One can only wonder how that might have changed our lives, but as the exact details are not known, it is hard to say.

At around this time, my mother had received a visit from a lady called Kathleen Fright, who, it transpired, was the daughter of Grandmother Heyman's sister, who was no longer alive. Her husband, Mr Fright, had been deputy governor of Walton prison in Liverpool, and my mother had met them when she went to stay in Liverpool with Aunty Flo (Cunningham) in the early days of her marriage to my father. Uncle Fright was a rather eccentric gentleman, who had retired from prison service and was living at Kingsnorth on the other side of Ashford. It was all very intriguing to discover relatives from my father's side, but of course, it was difficult to have any dialogue about him whenever they came to visit, even though they visited very infrequently, because of upsetting Bert. Kathleen worked as a proofreader with one of the local papers, as had our first lodger.

Things finally came to a head between Bert and me in about mid-1948. I had been to the pictures at the Odeon to see a particularly good film and for some reason had decided to have a seat in the circle rather than the stalls. This had cost me more. The following evening, having been told by Lionel (who worked for him) that he had seen me at the pictures, sitting in the circle, Bert verbally attacked me for being too high and mighty to sit in the cheaper seats. As usual, he worked himself up into a frenzy of temper that culminated in telling me 'to get out'. Never, during any of his previous outbursts had I responded, but on this occasion, I could not restrain myself. I said, 'Yes, I will get out'. To this day, I can remember the look of consternation on his and my mother's faces. And during the following weeks when I gave in my notice to Ms Butler and moved to Maidstone, he gave me no more verbal lashings.

My mother arranged for me to lodge with Mrs Gillam with whom she had lodged during her time in Maidstone.

Reflections—Two

Perhaps the most difficult part to understand during the 236 period is my mother's role. It is true to say that she found the whole domestic front hard going, and being tied down by two young children, first Barclay and then Chris, it was even harder. She had not been involved with the early years of either Peter or myself, and whilst she was slightly more involved with Maureen, it was Maureen, in the end, who was the one who really missed out at 236. Peter was about ten and I was thirteen when we moved there, but Maureen was still very young. She was three, coming up to four, when Barclay was born. She was the farmed out one. She was sent to Detling with Grandma and Aunty Kalla. In Charing, she was sent to a far-from-satisfactory babyminder. Two housekeepers followed for brief periods and then Maureen was sent back to Detling. There was also a period when Grandma took her to the Knowle farm. Subsequently, after I had left home, Francis and Bill, who had been living in the basement, moved to a house on the other side of Ashford, and Maureen lived with them for about a year. Of the three of us, Maureen was the one who suffered most from a lack of mothering by my mother.

It has been said of my mother that she was a good-time girl; certainly, she found domesticity pretty hard going. She loved nothing better than getting dressed up once a week and accompanying Bert to their favourite pub—The Wagon and Horses at Badlesmere and sometimes The Fox at Willesborough. As they got older, the boys and Maureen would be taken with them in the back of the lorry to The Wagon and Horses.

It was almost as though my mother was a split personality. Outside the home, she presented herself as 'county', wearing jodhpurs as though she was going riding. I think that part of Bert's dislike of me was that I represented a way of life which had been ours at Park Farm and which my mother still hankered after in the way she presented herself outside the home. Plus, of course, I knew that they were not married, and although I never alluded to this, I must have been a constant reminder of this by my presence.

What I still find hard to understand is how my mother could stand by and watch us receiving such treatment from Bert without intervening. In fact, she would often provoke situations that would incur his wrath. All this constant haranguing without being able to respond affected my ability to formulate a response. I carried around these bottled-up feelings all the time, feeling miserable and dejected. I loved my mother but did not like or understand her, and when I did at last reply to Bert's edict to get out, it left me feeling frightened at my own temerity but also greatly relieved.

23 London Road, Maidstone, Kent

Mrs Gillam, Monica's grandmother, was the landlady of this boarding house. When my mother had lodged with her, she had been tenant of an establishment lower down London Road—No. 7. Number 23 was a semi-detached property. The other side of this property (No. 21) was occupied by Mrs Gillam's daughter Olive, Olive's husband George, and their two children, Vivienne and Norman. Number 23 comprised a very large lounge, a bedroom, a living room, and kitchen on the ground floor and six bedrooms to the first and second floors plus bathroom. There was also a large basement.

I was to live as one of the family, an arrangement agreed to by my mother. I shared the ground floor bedroom with Monica and Aunty (Mrs Gillam). They had a double bed, and I had a single bed along the wall behind the bedroom door. The remaining rooms on the first and second floor were let out as bedsits on a mainly bed-and-breakfast basis, although some long-term tenants had evening meal and full board at the weekends.

My first priority was to find employment. I think I had set the ball rolling before I left home by responding to an advertisement for a secretary in a local newspaper. Then I attended the interview when I moved to Maidstone. This was at the branch office of a firm of printers—namely Kenrick & Jefferson, 27 Mote Road, Maidstone. I was duly offered the job, and so I commenced approximately eight years of very happy employment, working with people who became good colleagues and friends.

Monica, a year younger than me, was just finishing her schooling when I first moved to Maidstone, but she subsequently found a secretarial position at Oakwood Hospital. Aunty, a very cheerful and caring Yorkshire lady, was an excellent cook, and we were well looked after. We both came home from work for dinner during the lunch break, which involved, for me, a walk of about a mile to and fro. Then we came home for tea after work. I would knit, embroider, and read in the evenings, and at the weekends, Monica and I would clean the usually empty bedsits and make them ready for the occupants' return at the beginning of the week. This was done on Sunday mornings because on Saturday it was the ritual to go down to town. Olive, Vivienne, Aunty, Monica, and I went shopping, usually mooching around the clothes shops and then going for a coffee.

It was such an entirely different way of life to that I had left behind in Ashford, and I still felt quite bitter about the way I had been treated. Because of this, I did not go home until Christmas. However, once a week after work, I would catch the bus to Detling and have tea with Aunty Kalla, Ian, Jennifer, and Grandma, if she was there, and this routine continued throughout my years in Maidstone. Ian and Jennifer would make good use of my weekly visits to read them their bedtime story—usually Winnie the Pooh. I took the opportunity to catch up on the latest serial in *Women's Weekly*. I think I must have been a bit overzealous with this as Aunty Kalla gently remarked on one occasion that she would like to know whether I had lost my tongue! I would return to Maidstone on the nine o'clock bus, having thoroughly enjoyed my time in their company. Later on, I would spend the occasional weekend in Detling, going to church with the family on Sunday morning and then for a walk in the afternoon, after dinner. Aunty Kalla and Grandma had played such a significant and happy part in my early years at Park Farm that the unhappy years in between, whilst not put to rest, were to a degree, blotted out.

It was late July in 1948 when I commenced work with K&J. The firm occupied two rooms on the first floor of what had been a large private house. The rest of the building was used as offices by the firm of builders who owned the whole site. It was owned by two brothers—one an architect, who had his office opposite to K&J on the first floor and the other, who ran the day-to-day activities of the firm from offices on the ground floor. The building was enclosed by a brick wall, and the frontage was laid out by well-kept grass and flower beds which were a picture in the spring and summer months. I mention all this to convey what a peaceful setting I enjoyed in my new workplace.

I had been interviewed by Mr Redman, the branch manager. I subsequently met up with the two representatives, Harold Jenvey and Gordon Dymott, with whom I shared an office at the back of the building. Mr Redman's office was next to it on the front of the building. My role was to do the paperwork for the two reps, who came in on different days to put through their orders to Head Office; they both came in on Fridays to do their weekly expenses. Mr Redman would oversee all activities and dictate lengthy memos to Head Office (the factory was in West Bromwich in the Midlands) to support whatever action he recommended on either of the reps' patches. At the beginning, I had the only phone on my desk with an extension to Mr Redman, so when the reps wanted to use the phone, they had to do so from my desk. Later on, an extension was provided to each desk, but I still controlled the main phone and had to get their calls and then put them through which kept me quite busy on the days on which they were in the office.

Gordon Dymott had been moved from K&J's office in London to Maidstone, and he was living in a company property further up London Road. He and his wife were a lovely, middle-aged couple and were very musical. He was a talented pianist, and she had been an opera singer. In the first year or two, I was invited to their house for an evening meal on a few occasions. It was like going into a different world; they both dressed for dinner and everything was beautifully cooked and presented. Afterwards, they entertained their guests—Mrs Dymott sang and Gordon accompanied her. It was all so gracious. Unfortunately, they did not really take to life in Maidstone.

Harold Jenvey, a bachelor in his early forties, was a staid and determined gentleman. He was a good rep, who produced excellent sales figures on his patch, but he also applied the same vigour in ensuring that his office work always received priority over everyone else. He had a habit of not producing his work until the last minute, thus ensuring that I had to type flat out to finish it in time to catch the post. This was particularly true on a Friday when they were both in the office, and the relationship between the two—Gordon and Harold—would get a bit fraught on occasion.

Mr Redman, the branch manager, was a small, slight gentleman with twinkly eyes and a large moustache. To begin with, I was quite in awe of him; he could read Pitman's shorthand, and when dictating, he would keep an eye on my notes and point out that I could have used such and such a short form! More disconcertingly, he would often give notes that he had written in shorthand to decipher. Although, in all fairness, this did not cause me any problems, it was a bit unusual! He did not have good health—suffered with angina—and although he was on tablets to control the pain, at times it was obvious that these did not work too well. When I had been there for a while, he began to recount his experiences as a prisoner of war in Germany for a period of about three years. A lot of his ill health stemmed from then. Both he and Mrs Redman shared a love of gardening and grew all their vegetables. She was an excellent cook—a thoroughly motherly figure—who would ensure that Mr Redman did not overdo things on the work front.

They were both very kind to me during my years with K&J. They would invite me to their home for meals and would include me in their visits to the theatre in Maidstone. We usually went to a Gilbert and Sullivan opera performance, although, later on, we did degenerate into a Billy Cotton concert! One great highlight was being treated to the musical *Kiss Me, Kate* in London.

When I first commenced with K&J, I worked a five-and-a-half-day week, but shortly afterwards, it was reduced to five days and instead of meeting up with Monica, Aunty, and Olive in town, I was then able to have a more leisurely start to Saturday mornings.

There was a constant turnover of people staying at 23 London Road. George, husband to Olive next door, was a rep with Sharps' Toffee whose factory was at the bottom of London Road, alongside the Medway. He had put forward Aunty's and Olive's names for accommodation of trainee reps who came to the factory for training every six weeks. It was not uncommon to have three at a time, and quite often, because of scarcity of space, the lounge was press-ganged into use. Meals were always served in the main living room, adjacent to the kitchen at the back of the house, but since this related only to breakfast at staggered times, it did not pose a problem. There were one or two regulars, but on the whole, it was short-term letting. Thinking back, it provided an array of different characters over the years, some of whom became good friends.

Monica and I spent most of our leisure time together in the first year. She was having piano lessons, and I decided to do likewise. I did not persevere with practising my set lessons and dropped out after about six weeks, much to my shame. On our excursions into town on Saturdays, we would buy the latest popular record and play it endlessly on the gramophone in the lounge.

Eventually, the supply of Sharp's trainee reps came to an end and then followed a succession of females, apart from two or three male regulars. Two of these girls, working in Maidstone, became very good friends—Joy Batt and Ann Bourner. Joy was a police driver and Ann was a secretary; Joy came from Sellindge, near Ashford, where her parents farmed. Ann came from Cranbrook, where her parents also were farmers. Joy's interests were whist drives and bridge parties. Ann would join Monica and me in our various activities—the Star Ballroom on Saturday nights where the big bands of the time like Geraldo, Victor Silvester, Joe Loss, etc. entertained. We usually managed to find dancing partners for the evening. All three of us had passing boyfriends—nothing serious—it was all very light-hearted. Subsequently, Joy and I went to evening classes to improve our shorthand and typewriting speeds. We kept ourselves well occupied out of working hours.

All these activities, coupled with the social side of work, made the time go quickly. Around Christmas, the K&J Maidstone staff went up to London to attend a dinner dance organised by the branch manager of the London office. I usually went with Mr and Mrs Redman in their car, and it was always a very pleasant occasion, putting faces to names of people with whom we liaised on the phone. I was wrong to have said earlier on in this narrative that I went home for the first Christmas. In fact, I now remember that I went to Detling. On Boxing Day, the whole family spent the day with Uncle Alec, Aunty Edie, Janet, and Bill at Harpshall Farm, a walking distance of about a mile from Detling village. By this time, Uncle Ted was home, having been demobbed from the army. When staying in Detling, Grandma would quite often meet me in Maidstone, and we would have lunch together. It would always have to be the best restaurant available, and she would choose the most expensive item on the menu on the basis that it had to be good value! And a tip was left, discreetly placed under a plate.

When I first arrived at 23, I was soon made aware of the problems Aunty had with her legs. She suffered from very bad varicose veins. Notwithstanding this, she and Olive would go down to town shopping every weekday morning, sometimes catching the tram back again. However, as time went by, her legs became a lot worse, and she would have bleeds which were quite frightening, and on one occasion she was confined to bed for about ten days. During this period, Monica and I took over the preparation of breakfasts and Olive would then take over. Because the doctor was visiting, my bed was moved to the lounge, which became my bedroom for a few weeks, and then I finally shared a bedsit with Joy.

I did not really start to go home to Ashford until about mid-1950, when work had commenced on building a two-storey extension at the back where the lean-to shed had been. This comprised a kitchen and a bathroom. The family were trying to cope with the incredible mess that the builders were causing for about a year, and when it was finally all finished, there was quite a lot of dissatisfaction with various aspects. However, it must be said that the bathroom was a very welcome addition! The airing cupboard contained the hot-water tank, heated by the Raeburn stove in the kitchen below, which provided constant warmth. I really blotted my copybook by accidentally dropping the plastic toilet seat, causing it to crack. It became quite a hazardous business to sit on the toilet for quite a few years afterwards, because the seat was not renewed. I had not realised until writing about it that there was a somewhat ironic sense of justice about this sometimes-painful outcome! Sneaky!

This improvement in the living arrangements motivated my mother to start decorating, and I went home more often to give a hand, stripping walls, etc. The hall and stairwells had about five different layers of wallpaper, and it was a mammoth task to get it all off. Even Bert turned to with an axe used as a scraper. Someone came in to do the papering. I went to Ashford with my mother to choose wallpaper for the attic bedrooms and at the same time bought material for curtains and bedspreads, which I made by hand since we did not own a sewing machine. In all fairness to my mother, the whole house was much more comfortable than before and easier for her to cope with. I suppose Chris and Barclay cannot remember it as it was before this work had been done.

My relationship with Bert had improved since I left 236. I cannot say that I enjoyed being in his company, but certainly he did not give me any aggro. I used to enjoy the boys, Chris and Barclay, and when at home for the weekend, I would look after them while my mother and Bert went out on Friday evenings. This would involve bathing them, washing their hair, and cutting their nails, something which Barclay hated. At one stage, they were both sleeping in the same attic bedroom. Having put them to bed following the above ritual, I heard some noise. On investigating what was causing the noise, I found them having a pillow fight; one of the feather pillows had burst, and the whole bedroom was covered in feathers. I cannot remember the outcome, but this was just one of the pranks they got up to. The saying 'Boys will be boys' was not wasted on these two!

It was on one of these weekends at home when I specifically went to help my mother. Aunty Kalla was recuperating from an operation, so Ian and Grandma came to stay at 236 for a week. I think Jennifer must have stayed elsewhere. At the end of the week, we were returning them both to Bexhill-on-Sea, to where the family had moved some time previously, en route to an ice show in Brighton. This was quite an occasion—the whole family going to an ice show! It was the mode of transport that did not quite fit the image! The back of the lorry had been covered with a tarpaulin. One of the armchairs from the living room was lifted into the well for Grandma and two bench seats were placed along each side for the rest of us. So, having helped Grandma to get up the wooden steps into the lorry and settled her into her armchair, well wrapped in blankets, the rest of us, apart from Mum, Chris, and Bert who were in the front cab, settled ourselves onto the bench seats. Also included were Dusky and the steps. And off we went—rather exposed to the elements because the tarpaulin was open at the end. I will never forget the expression on Grandma's face—coping with being exposed to the view of following cars with Dusky barking all the time! Grandma was duly unloaded at Bexhill-on-Sea, together with Ian, and on we went to the ice show. We had very good seats, and the whole show was spectacular. However, when we returned to the lorry at the end, it was to find a very disgruntled mother complaining because Dusky had bitten her son. Quite what the boy had been doing was hard to understand because Dusky was tied up in the back of the lorry, but I think a small amount of money changed hands to sort this out. Quite a day!

On the work front with K&J, there had been quite a change. To begin with, Gordon Dymott had resigned and moved to live in Worthing in Sussex. He had been replaced by John Saunders from Leicester. He moved with his wife and family into the company property vacated by the Dymotts. Then subsequently, another rep was taken on (Fred Tatham) because of the increasing need for K&J products in the area covered by Maidstone Branch Apart from the printing side of K&J's business, they also sold business systems and equipment. With a sales force of three, Mr Redman's supervisory role was quite demanding. In an effort to provide an instant service to customers of things like envelopes, paper, etc., a further room was leased in the attic of the premises and was set up as a stock room. I became packer-in-chief when the need arose, having been shown how to pack neatly by Mr Redman. A photo of me appeared in the K&J monthly newsletter, submitted by Mr Redman, who was very proud of his brainchild—not me, the concept! There was strong competition between the countrywide branches of K&J to achieve the best sales figures every month, particularly between our nearest branch in London and ourselves, and then within the branch between the three reps.

John and Audrey Saunders became good friends. They had a young family of two when they first arrived (Mandy and Jonathan) and then had another child (Jamie). Audrey found it quite difficult to settle down to life in Maidstone, and I was enlisted to babysit to enable her and John to get out together. Quite often, Monica would join me and then Ann. We had some good times together, and our friendship lasted for many years. Fred Tatham, when he first joined K&J, was engaged, but then subsequently, he and Evelyn were married. Within the office, John and Fred became good mates. Harold, the longest-serving of the three and a bachelor, did not mix socially with the team other than at organised work get-togethers.

In the early days of living in Maidstone, I joined the Young Conservatives Association, who had premises just down the road from 23. I cannot remember how this came about or who introduced me, but it did open up a wider circle of acquaintances. I was persuaded to take minutes of the meetings whilst the post holder was away, but on her return, I gladly relinquished this rather arduous job. I was not a regular attender but did enjoy the social side—the annual dinner dance.

Like most young ladies, I enjoyed being able to buy fashionable clothes particularly since the shops were full of such a variety in the euphoria of the postwar era. When the new look came in, I bought various things which included a bright yellow half-length jacket with swing-back and a pencil-slim brown skirt which had a buttoned vent at the back. To walk comfortably, it was necessary to undo the first two or three buttons of the vent, but I stretched things to the limit when, on lifting my leg to board a bus, there was a ping-ping and three buttons flew off at the feet of the male passenger boarding behind me! He bent down and retrieved two of the three buttons and calmly handed them to me, apologizing for the fact that the third could not be found! I did not follow my usual pattern of going upstairs but remained downstairs on the bus—with a very red face and acutely aware that the next hurdle was getting off and exposing a greatly extended back vent in my skirt. 'Pride comes before a fall' very aptly fitted this situation!

During my time at 23, I had various holidays the first of which was with Monica, to her mother and stepfather's home in Devon. They lived on the outskirts of Dartmoor, and they were looking for a house nearer to the school where George was headmaster. We visited quite a few very nice properties with them and thoroughly enjoyed this. I cannot remember exactly where they were living at the time, but of course, I was no stranger to Devon, as I had been evacuated to Torquay during the war. And I was still entranced by the beautiful beaches and clear blue seawater.

Coincidentally, my second holiday was to Torquay, this time in the company of a friend from my Technical College days—Peggy Bean. Quite how we met up again eludes me, but we spent a very pleasant week in a hotel in Babbacombe. It was almost like 'ships passing in the night' because after the holiday I did not see Peggy again. I suppose our everyday lives took over; at the time of our holiday, she was about to get engaged and I suppose she married subsequently.

I spent a further holiday at Detling with Aunty Kalla and Uncle Ted. My holiday dates were always determined by K&J; the factory in West Bromwich closed down for two weeks during the summer months, and the branches also closed for the same period. Aunty Kalla spoilt me rotten, as they say! Breakfast in bed every morning and loads of reading matter to hand. I managed to read a collection of Shakespeare's major works, which were contained in a leather-bound volume. This had been a farewell present to Aunty Kalla in her teaching days. One day was spent going round Whipsnade Zoo, mainly for the benefit of Ian and Jennifer, but nevertheless, it was thoroughly enjoyed by us all. I was greatly impressed that Uncle Ted would not allow me to pay for my expenses, which included the train fare and entrance to the zoo. As was usual in most homes during the period, the household duties were allocated to a different day of the week; Monday was usually washday and Tuesday was for ironing, which by this time had been made more easy by the use of an electric iron rather than the old method of using flat irons. Wednesday (or possibly Thursday) was baking day, and Aunty Kalla introduced me to pastry—and cake-making methods during this holiday. Friday was housecleaning day. Whatever activity took place, it was always finished in the morning, and the afternoons were clear for whatever leisure pursuit we decided on. Mealtimes were very organised; breakfast, dinner usually at midday, and then tea at around five o'clock. I suppose, because it was so reminiscent of life at Park Farm, my sense of contentment was twofold. I thoroughly enjoyed this time with the family in Detling, and my knowledge of Winnie the Pooh and Christopher Robin was greatly improved by reading bedtime stories to Ian and Jennifer!

My twenty-first birthday was celebrated at Detling. Aunty Kalla had invited me there together with Monica, and we went over by bus after work. The table was groaning with food—lovely cakes, trifles, and sandwiches. My mother was also there and gave me my present—a watch—with which I was delighted. I had money from Grandma and Uncle Alec, who popped in during the evening to give this to me. I remember being very surprised and grateful for this because he had always been on the periphery of close relations, and I was surprised that he would have known about my birthday. This money contributed very greatly to my being able to afford my fourth holiday.

Joy and I had been talking for a while about going on holiday together to the continent. And our plans finally came to fruition when we went to Belgium on an organised trip. I travelled down to Sellindge and spent the night with Joy's parents. In the early morning, Joy's sister drove us down to Dover to catch the cross-Channel ferry—my first experience of going to sea. I felt very queasy and sat on deck in the fresh air for most of the crossing. I cannot now remember which port we went into—possibly Zeebrugge—where we were met by a coach and were conveyed to our hotel in Bruge. Joy and I shared a twin-bedded room at the top of rather narrow and windy stairs. The building was very old and the plumbing equally so! Every quarter of an hour during the night, we were serenaded by the many chiming clocks in the vicinity. This took a bit of getting used to, but the whole atmosphere of the place was charming and old-worldly. Also included was my first introduction to continental breakfasts. We went on various coach trips. We visited Ghent to see the Cathedral; the Mennin Gate with its interminable list of those killed in the First World War and then to various of the war cemetries in the same area; Brussels, and Antwerp, where I think it was we visited the Ruben's gallery; the Isle of Walcheren to see the wonderful displays of lace in the markets; and Lille in northern France, where we visited a very interesting museum.

There was little time for relaxation, although we spent one day browsing around Bruge and a bit of time on the beach of a neighbouring seaside resort. We made friends with another girl on the coach trips; she came from London and was instrumental, following our return to the UK, in booking the three of us into a performance of *Swan Lake* and *The Nutcracker Suite* ballets at Sadlers Wells. Plus the musical, *Porgie and Bess*, but this was cancelled because the American cast were prohibited from performing in this country.

Arrangements had been made for me to meet up with Grandma at 236 on my return as I was to accompany her by coach to Wolverhampton to stay with Aunty May. My visit was twofold; K&J were celebrating the seventy-fifth anniversary of the founding of the company on 2 October 1953, and all personnel from the branches were invited to attend at the factory in West Bromwich. We were first given a guided tour of all the different departments, very interesting but too numerous to mention! Then we had tea in the canteen, and then we went back to our hotels to dress for dinner, which was held in a massive hall that must have accommodated about two hundred and fifty people. We were then ferried by a coach to a Midnight Matinee held at The Tower Cinema in West Bromwich. The directors of the company welcomed us from the stage and then followed a very comprehensive and enjoyable programme of entertainment. By the time of our return to the hotel, we were all pretty tired but thoroughly appreciative of being included in such a spectacular celebration.

I was still on holiday so did not accompany the rest of the branch team back to Maidstone. Instead, Uncle Jim (Grandma's brother) picked me up from the hotel and took me back to Wolverhampton, where I rejoined Grandma at Aunty May's. From there, we visited Aunty Min, Uncle Harry, and the boys at the Knowle farm, the first time I had seen them since staying there during the early part of the war. Ena and husband Aubrey invited us to their home in Wolverhampton for an evening meal by which time I had developed a really heavy cold and was unable to do justice to their hospitality. However, it was just lovely to meet up with them again.

Uncle Jim drove Grandma and me back to Kent. He had lived and worked in Canada most of his life following the First World War, but following the death of his wife in the late 1940s, he came back to the UK for extended visits. I mention this because he always brought back his large left-hand drive American car and had a habit of forgetting and going round roundabouts the right-hand way, which was a bit disconcerting to his passengers, although I must say that Grandma was completely unfazed! However, I was safely returned to Maidstone, Aunty was introduced to Uncle Jim, and then off he went with Grandma to return her to Aunty Kalla!

When travelling home for the weekend, I always travelled by bus. Although it was only about twenty to twenty-five miles, the journey took about an hour, going through all the villages on its route—Harrietsham, Charing, and Lenham. A chance remark by me to my mother about the possibility of learning to drive resulted in her arranging with one of the men who worked for Bert—namely Lionel—to give me lessons. So I started the learning process by driving back to Maidstone on a Sunday evening in Lionel's car. I did not go home every weekend, so this was usually on a fortnightly basis. On one weekend at home, Lionel decided that I needed more experience in traffic. So to Ashford we went and stopped at traffic lights at the top of Station Road. Prior to turning right down East Hill, when I revved up before releasing the brake, I must have over-revved, and instead of going forward, the car rolled back onto the bus behind! Lionel took over but could not get the car to move, so he and the bus driver pushed the car while I steered the car over to the top of East Hill where it had to be left. I caught the bus home. It subsequently transpired that by over-revving, according to Lionel, I had broken the already cracked half shaft. I was very embarrassed by the whole episode, and that was the end of driving lessons. Poor Lionel! He certainly got the raw end of the deal.

During my time at 23, I had various short-lived friendships with young men, who I met either as boarders at 23 or at the Young Conservatives or occasionally at the Star Ballroom on a Saturday evening. One of these was Johnny, a pilot stationed at West Malling RAF base, and so I went in his company to various dances held there. Aunty was very good and occasionally invited him back to 23 for an evening meal, but then he was posted and that was the end of Johnny. Another good friend was Frank Matta; he had an estate agent's business in Maidstone, and at the weekends, we would go out for the day in his car, together with another lad and his girlfriend, visiting places of historical interest and then going for a meal. There were other acquaintances, but on the whole, we tended to go out together in groups—Monica, Joy, Ann, and myself—to the pictures or shows. Of course, Joy and I went to evening classes.

Following our holiday in Belgium, Joy and I had felt it difficult to settle down to life at 23. Joy went home every weekend and did not receive the full board for which she was paying, and although I did not go away as frequently, I just felt the need to be more independent. So we decided to find accommodation which the two of us could share. Aunty had been very kind to me, but I think I can say in all honesty that I helped her a great deal by cleaning with Monica and also by keeping the lawns and flower beds under control during the summer months. I think, in some ways, it was probably a relief to her, because by then, she had given up providing meals for the boarders and was just letting the rooms as bedsits.

I think it was Joy, who located our new accommodation, and after viewing it, we decided to take it on.

The White Horse Inn, Bearsted, Maidstone, Kent

The frontage of the White Horse Inn overlooked the extensive village green, but since it was situated on a corner, the side of the premises faced two or three small shops on the other side of the road. It was a very old and charming building. It was the kind of place where, when you use the old English word *hostelry,* it fits into one's image of such establishments. It even had an unused stable block to reinforce this impression.

Joy and I rented two rooms on the first floor. The rooms were situated over the public bar. We had our own staircase entrance accessed from a narrow passage at the back of the bars and were able to bolt the door behind us at the bottom of the stairs to repel invaders. At the top of the stairs, another door opened into our living area—a large beamed room with a fireplace—comfortably furnished with old-style furniture and a table and chairs in front of the window. One corner of the room was curtained off, and behind the curtains, there was a kitchen table, a cooker, and food cupboard. No sink. All water had to be carried from the bathroom and slops had to be taken back there for disposal. Through a door to the adjacent bedroom, which housed two single beds, there were a chest of drawers and a wardrobe. It was very quaint and in many ways rather impractical, but both Joy and I were bowled over by the sheer charm of the place.

The owner of the White Horse was Mrs Ben Brooks—known to all and sundry as Aunty Ben. She was a large lady, always well coiffured, dressed in twin sets and tweedy skirts, and was never without her strings of pearls. She was assisted in the running of the establishment by Lorna, whose surname I never got to know. Aunty Ben's husband had died many years before, and she had become known as Aunty Ben rather than by her own Christian name, which again, I never got to know. She was an amazing no-nonsense character, very shrewd and discerning but with a large heart.

A door from our bedroom went into a wide corridor, and opposite was Aunty Ben's bedroom. Carrying on down the corridor, there was a further bedroom on the right, which was occupied, soon after our arrival, by a couple; he had recently left the air force and was working in Maidstone. The corridor branched right, and Lorna's bedroom was here, then the bathroom and a further bedroom. Without turning right, the corridor carried on to the main staircase, which led down into the large front entrance hall of the accommodation. Behind this lay Aunty Ben's snug, cosy living room, which did not have a window, and it was only served with daylight through glass panels in the two doors. However, there were copious table lamps on all the time and usually a roaring coal fire. The whole effect was Dickensian.

Beyond this, through a maze of passageways to the cavernous kitchen, was the large hall, which in Mr Brooks' day had been used for local celebrations, whist drives, etc. It was no longer used, and it had become the dumping ground for old furniture from the living accommodation. The kitchen would have accommodated an army of cooks, but now the only people to use it were Aunty Ben and Lorna, and the new couple. Having seen the kitchen, Joy and I understood and appreciated our curtained off kitchen area in our living room!

We soon settled down to a routine, taking it in turns to wash up after our limited breakfast in the mornings. Use of the bathroom was by rote but since this only related to four of us, Aunty Ben and Lorna not surfacing until after our departure for work, the system worked quite well. We walked to the top of the lane to the main road—about half a mile—to catch the bus. In the better weather, we would use our bikes—about two and a half miles. This was fine while going to work as it was mainly downhill but not so good on the return journey. Quite often, we would get a lift from the couple who also lived at the White Horse.

Shortly after our move, Aunty Kalla and Uncle Ted also moved to Bexhill-on-Sea so my weekly visits to them finished. However, once a week I would go to 23 London Road after work and have tea with Aunty and Monica before going to evening classes. Joy and I were both intent on improving our shorthand and typing speeds. Joy always went home at the weekends after work on Fridays, returning on Sunday evenings. I thoroughly enjoyed having the place to myself. Aunty Ben quite often invited me to have Sunday lunch with her when her gentleman friend was not available. He was a portly bank manager with a Jaguar car, and she enjoyed being taken out and about, whilst he, in turn, enjoyed being wined and dined in her inner sanctum after church on Sundays. Aunty Ben was an excellent cook, and working with her gave me some very useful tips. I joined her for Sunday morning service at Bearsted Church. When she found out that I had not been confirmed, she set the wheels in motion for this to happen. I was subsequently confirmed by the Bishop of Dover on 18 May 1955 at the grand old age of twenty-four. I remember how pleased Aunty Kalla was to know that this had taken place.

On three consecutive weekends, I suggested to my mother that I would have Maureen and the boys to stay. Maureen was the first, travelling from Ashford by bus, and I met her at the bus stop at the top of the lane. From her account, I do not think I entertained her very well, because in the evening I had to leave her alone in bed with her crayons and picture book whilst I helped out in the bar below. I would wash the glasses when they were very busy. The following weekend, Barclay was dropped off by Peter, who was travelling on his motorbike to join up for his National Service. I was allowed to use the adjoining bedroom so that Barclay could have my bed, and the following weekend Chris arrived. I do recall that Fred Tatham (K&J rep), was very kind and took us out and about, when both Barclay and Chris stayed.

In the early days of our move, Monica and Aunty Gillam came to tea, to see how we were faring. With the fire lit, the living room soon warmed up, and I think they were suitably impressed, although the kitchen facility (or lack of facility) caused raised eyebrows!

During the week, Joy and I would make sandwiches to take with us for lunch, but on return in the evening, we would have a stew. This would start off as fresh on Monday evenings and then last until Thursday by adding more ingredients (usually vegetables) every evening! It certainly did not tax our culinary skills!

Part of Joy's need and my need to improve our shorthand and typing speeds was motivated by the possibility of working abroad. Joy had already given up her job as a police driver and was working in a secretarial position at Police Headquarters in Maidstone. We regularly bought a copy of the Pitman's Journal to improve our shorthand skills and came across an advertisement by the Crown Agents—secretaries with definitive shorthand and typing speeds required by the Nigerian Government. We were very taken with this, and we mulled it over and finally made the decision to 'go for it'.

However, in the meantime, two things happened which upset the apple cart for me. While running for the bus home from work in very high heels, I twisted my ankle very badly. By the time I reached home, my ankle had ballooned, and I was in acute pain. Aunty Ben insisted on calling the doctor, who in turn insisted on bedrest for at least a week. Aunty Ben then took charge. I was moved into her bedroom, into her massive bed, and meals were delivered on a tray. Poor Joy was left to her own devices food-wise. This state of affairs lasted for about ten days before I could confidently put my foot to the ground, and as I remember, it was two weeks before I returned to work.

Then, I met Patrick. He had joined the Saturday morning coffee group in Maidstone. He was training as a pilot in the Fleet Air Arm based at Valley, in Anglesey and would join the group spasmodically as and when he was on leave—he was very dashing in his uniform. We began to date regularly and write to each other while he was away. He bought a little car with a buggy seat at the back and would suddenly turn up at the White Horse, having secured a forty-eight-hour pass, most of which was spent on travelling to and from Valley. We had a good time together. On one occasion, he wanted to put in more hours on his private licence, and I accompanied him to Rochester Airport and sat on the floor at the back of the plane while he did circuit and bumps with an instructor. It was not the most comfortable way to be introduced to flying, but nevertheless, exciting. He took me to tea to his mother's house—she lived just outside Maidstone—a nice Irish lady.

It was at this time that the opportunity arose for Joy and me to apply for a secretarial job in Nigeria. Because of my attachment to Patrick, I did not want to proceed with this; she, however, did apply, and she was accepted. I felt quite bad about not going with her since we had worked towards this goal for so long, but in all fairness to Joy, it did not dampen her enthusiasm for what lay ahead. We had been good friends for a long time but did not share the same interests in our leisure time. Joy had one particular good friend, who accompanied her to whist drives and bridge parties, and since she always went home at the weekends, apart from evening classes, we did not share the same interests. Perhaps, because of this, we were good flatmates.

There was no difficulty in finding someone else to share the flat with. Ann Bourner joined me; she was a year or two younger, vivacious, and full of life. We got on well together. We mixed in the same circle of friends, although, by this time Ann was very committed to a lad called John Walters, who was in the RAF, training as a pilot. I was invited to spend a weekend with Ann at her home in Cranbrook, and we had a lovely time. Afterwards, Ann relayed to me that her mother was very pleased that she had teamed up with such a nice and sensible person! Praise indeed!

I gradually began to realise that Patrick was not committed to a long-term relationship. He wanted a trophy girlfriend to have fun with when he came home, someone who fitted in with his image of a dashing pilot. He was not particularly popular with the rest of the Saturday-morning gang and, he could be quite moody if he was not the centre of attention. Reluctantly, but dare I say, sensibly, I stopped seeing him on a regular basis, much regretting that I had not gone ahead and joined Joy in Nigeria.

Now, in the middle of 1955, I began to take stock of my life. I had, by then, been working for K&J for over seven years, and whilst I was perfectly happy there, it was all getting a bit stale. Mr Redman's health had deteriorated to the extent that he only worked part-time, and the thought of Harold Jenvey becoming the branch manager was not a happy one. Socially, I became good friends with Gordon Knight who was a rep with one of the Maidstone breweries. He was a Mason, and so I had my first introduction to a ladies' evening, when I accompanied him to the Young Farmers' Annual Ball and the Young Conservatives Dinner Dance. These functions called for full evening dress, and I thoroughly enjoyed all this. However, having borrowed my mother's white, rabbit evening jacket to attend one of these functions, Gordon was a bit put out to find that it had moulted over his black dinner jacket as I got into the car alongside him!

I would go home for the weekend about once a month with a suitcase of washing. My mother, quite incredibly, had become involved in the logging business! Every Saturday morning, Bert delivered logs round and about in Willesborough, and my mother accompanied him, humping sacks of logs on her back from the lorry to delivery point. I could not understand why she would want to do this. It must have imposed such a strain on her physically. Although she much preferred the outdoor life and went out to work with Bert in the woods, this seemed a step too far.

By that time, Maureen was fifteen, Barclay was eleven, and Chris was eight. I have often wondered since then as to how I fitted into the boys' perspective of a family. They had seen little of me since I left home in 1948. Maureen and I had spent more time together, but because of the conditions prevailing in the home at the time and also because of her frequent absences when she was farmed out, bless her, we were not able to be close sisters. Peter had remained at home until going into the army to do his National Service. Both the boys thought the world of him, and when he met and married Eileen in September 1955, I remember it being said that Chris had camped out on the doorstep of their home, not wanting to be parted from Peter.

I had been corresponding with Joy since her departure to Nigeria. She was enjoying life on the coast and this fed into my feelings of discontent that I was not going anywhere. Lovely as Bearsted was, with cricket matches on the village green on Saturdays in the summer, the fund-raising fêtes, and flower-arranging at church with Aunty Ben, I felt that I was missing out. This prompted me into applying to the Crown Agents for a secretarial position with the Nigerian Government in Lagos, to join Joy.

I was selected for interview in about October 1955. Ann accompanied me to the Crown Agents offices on Millbank in London. Armed with my shorthand and typing certificates, I nervously presented myself, very apprehensive that I would have to take tests. However, it turned out to be a very pleasant interview where I was asked about my previous secretarial experience and my understanding of what life would be like in Nigeria, which, thanks to Joy, I was able to answer quite competently. I was given a brief medical and told that I would be contacted in about six weeks' time.

It was such a relief to get this behind me. In a state of euphoria on my part, Ann and I celebrated by going to see *The Pyjama Game*, which was running in London at the time. I think the male lead was Edmund Hockeridge. We also had a small shopping session in C&A!

Then it was back to Bearsted and the normality of everyday life. And then, at about the beginning of December, a letter arrived from The Crown Agents, advising that I had been appointed as a secretary/typist, on a salary of £570 plus inducement allowance of £180 p.a. This compared very favourably with my salary from K&J of £8 weekly. I did not receive full confirmation until 2 February 1956, and this letter gave the date for my flight as 28 February 1956. It also listed the requirement for various vaccinations—smallpox, yellow fever, etc., and the need to commence taking an antimalarial drug (Paludrine) five days prior to leaving this country.

I had already put in my notice to K&J and received some very nice letters from the directors and the managers, thanking me for my services over a period of about seven years. My position was advertised. When I left, the position was taken by a friend I had known through the Young Conservatives. Ann decided to leave the flat at the White Horse when I left, and she boarded with John and Audrey Saunders. So there were quite a lot of emotional farewells to be made. I actually finished work with K&J halfway through February, taking my two weeks' due leave to enable me to prepare for the move. I went home for this period to sort everything out. I had received a long list of items I would need in Nigeria, which included a pith helmet and a hip bath! Thank goodness, Joy advised me not to take out other than light clothes, sheets, and towels since I could buy all other necessities there. Before leaving Bearsted, I had received £60 clothing allowance from the Crown Agents, and I had bought plenty of cotton items (rather than nylon), particularly underwear and dresses. I managed to acquire a tin trunk—cannot remember from where—and this was duly packed and despatched to go out by sea. It was a very busy fortnight.

And so, departure day dawned. John and Audrey Saunders, together with Ann, came to see me off at Victoria Coach Station where I was met by a Crown Agents representative with instructions for my journey. Then, I was onto the coach to Heathrow and a new life.

Reflections—Three

It is easier to look back and pinpoint how events were life changing rather than recognise them as they are taking place. The whole of the Maidstone and Bearsted era had the same theme running through; my employment with K&J, which was the bedrock of everyday life, working with people who became such good friends. My confidence had improved considerably. This was further enhanced by mixing with a wide circle of people at 23 London Road and the added closer companionship of Monica, Joy, and Ann. We all got on so well, and it was such a contrast to how things had been at home in Ashford.

When I moved to Bearsted, there was Aunty Ben. She must have decided that I needed looking after! She did not in any way try and control but was always there for a chinwag to put the world to rights. And then, of course, Aunty Kalla and Grandma. Being in regular contact with them again brought into focus so many happy years at Park Farm that it tended to blot out the dreary and unhappy times in between.

Perhaps the only downside was the knowledge that although things had improved at home—the house was a more comfortable and manageable place—my mother's role was a hard one. She went out to work with Bert in the woods, returning in the evening to cook a dinner and prepare the meal for the evening, followed by the endless sandwich-making for lunch the next day. 'You make your bed and you lie on it' is an apt description of how things had turned out for her. At this stage, I think she did have help in the house once a week, but there is no doubt that when I left home and then eventually Maureen, the full brunt on the domestic front fell on her shoulders. Because of this, her health suffered considerably.

All in all, I consider that I was very lucky to have had such wonderful Grandparents and Aunty Kalla to nurture and guide me through the early years which provided me with the strength of character to cope with the unhappy times. And the seven or so happy years in Maidstone and Bearsted reinforced this and enabled me to face the new challenge of life in Nigeria.

KENT EDUCATION COMMITTEE

Headmistress:

Miss M. M. Butler, B.A.

North County Modern Girls' School,
Mabledon Avenue,
ASHFORD, Kent.

Telephone: Ashford 776.

9th July, 1948.

I have pleasure in testifying as to the character
and capability of Miss J. Heyman, who commenced duty
here as Clerical Assistant at the beginning of Autumn
Term 1947, this being her first post after completing
three years training at Ashford County Technical School
for Girls.

Miss Heyman is an extremely capable girl, with a
pleasing manner.   She is a careful book-keeper, and an
accurate shorthand typist, showing a ready aptitude for
office routine, and a pleasant way of welcoming visitors
to the school and answering the telephone.   She has
continued to attend Evening Classes and has recently
passed the R.S.A. Intermediate Typewriting Examination
and R.S.A. 80 words a minute Shorthand Examination.
Since passing these she has taken the R.S.A. Advanced
Typewriting Examination, and will shortly be taking a
Shorthand Examination for 100 words a minute.

Miss Heyman shows great promise, and I am confident
that, if she continues to develop as she has done during
her first year in employment, she could become a most
valuable Secretary.   I regret that she is moving to
Maidstone and must therefore leave her present post.
I shall miss her, and have no hesitation in recommending
her as a trustworthy, conscientious girl possessing both
character and intelligence.

(Signed)   .........M.R.Butler

Headmistress.

k J

WEST BROMWICH · STAFFS
PHONE 1001
Office of the Chairman

AWK   1 February 1956

Miss P Heyman
Maidstone

Dear Miss Heyman

I have to-day seen the Form 611B that has come
~~through to say that you will be leaving our~~
employment on 17 February and I am interested
to see that you have chosen such a completely different
sphere of activity from that which you have previously
pursued

I hope that you may find Nigeria lives up to what you
expect it to be but while in many ways you will find it
very strange in probably a variety of ways I can quite
appreciate that it will be an experience you would not
willingly wish to miss

I hope that you will enjoy your new work and be happy in
it but you will understand that K&J will be very sorry to
lose you and in saying that I speak not only for the
Maidstone staff but for us here   For over 7 years you
have been a great standby at Maidstone and I would like to
thank you for what you have done while you have been with
us and perhaps sometimes while you are far away you will
spare a thought for those you have known in England

                    Yours sincerely

                    A WYNN KENRICK

Kenrick Jefferson Limited

PRINTERS

C H A I R M A N:
A. WYNN KENRICK, J.P.
MANAGING DIRECTOR:
T. JEFFERSON COTTRELL
DIRECTORS:
A. COLIN KENRICK
E. PETER KENRICK
T. KENNETH JEFFERSON

9 Cavendish Square
London W1

TELEPHONE: LANGHAM 8721/2/3

GET HOLD OF

TRADE MARK

OUR REF.	YOUR REF	DATE
L/RC		13 February 1956

Miss P J Heyman
Kenrick & Jefferson Ltd
27 Mote Road
Maidstone
Kent

Dear Miss Heyman

Thank you very much for your letter and enclosure

I did hear a rumour of the possibility of you going
to Nigeria - all our best women seem to be going
there nowadays!- and I know how much Mr Redman will
miss your help at Maidstone

I would like to wish you everything that is good in
your new venture, I am sure you will find your new
environment very interesting indeed

On behalf of all at our London House let me wish you
Bon Voyage and all possible success

With kindest regards

Yours sincerely

Ralph Colvin

*how many will be leaving from
Maidstone — any idea of Mr*

Redman

KENRICK & JEFFERSON LTD.
PRINTERS
WESTBROMWICH, ENGLAND

JB   16 February 1956

Miss P J Heyman
MAIDSTONE

Dear Miss Heyman

I have waited until to-day before writing to wish
you happiness and success in the interesting new
appointment which you are taking up and I am sure
you are going to have a thrilling and fascinating
experience

Don't be surprised if you see familiar K&J labels
when you get out to Nigeria   We have quite a number
of customers in Lagos, Ibadan, Ijebu-Ode and in smaller
places and if you fly out to Lagos, which I think you
may well do, almost the first building you see - the
Ikeja Arms Hotel - at the Airport, buys its letter
headings from K&J

You will be greatly missed at Maidstone and by some
of us at West Bromwich too, and I want to take this
opportunity of thanking you for the good work you
have done for us at Maidstone

                    Yours sincerely

                    J Blanchard
                    SALES MANAGER

Views of Park Farm
1930's

Ernest Cooper Heyman,
Peter and Jean's father

Wedding of Cooper Heyman
and Marjorie Hooker

GRANDMA GRANDAD and JEAN
at Park Farm

JEAN standing by the
Well Cover in the garden of Park Farm

GRANDAD Hooker tending the
sheep at Park Farm

MUM AUNTY KALLA
and JEAN at Park Farm

MUM and KALLA
cherry picking at Park Farm

AUNTY KALLA MUM PETER
and JEAN

Peter and Jean
standing in The Larches
at Park Farm

John Harwood, Peter and Jean
on the beach at Whitstable

Jean at Throwley Vicarage

Mr & Mrs Harwood, John and Jean
on camping holiday

Jean ans Aunty Kalla
in the garden at Park Farm

John Harwood and Jean
on running-board of Singer

KALLA and JEAN
at Vicarage

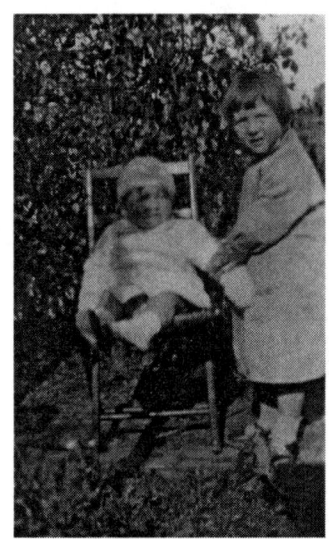

PETER and JEAN
one and three years old

JEAN and PETER
five and three years old

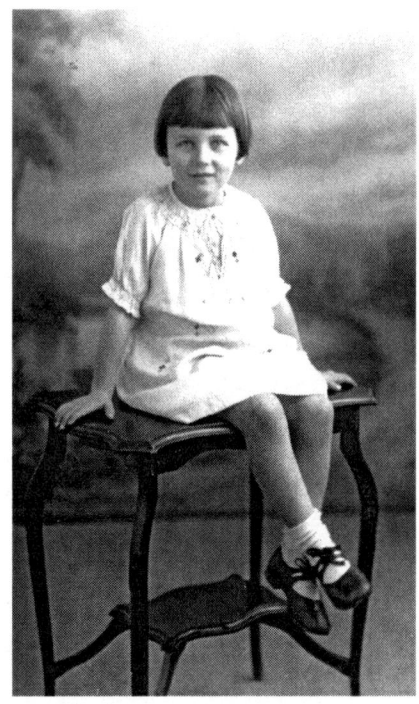

JEAN—six years old

PETER with MAUREEN'S father

JEAN PETER JANNET and BILL
at Harpshall Farm

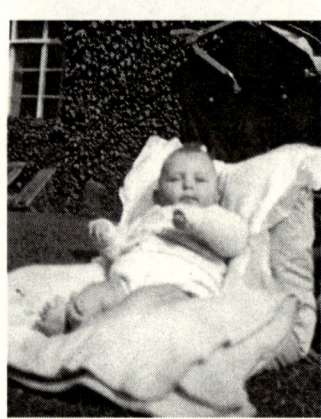

MAUREEN at The Knowle

JEAN MAUREEN and PETER
at The Knowle

JEAN at The Knowle
Age 10 years

Uncle TED Aunty KALLA IAN and JENNIFER
at Detling

GRANDMA and UNCLE JIM THOMPSON

AUNTY MIM at The Knowle

ARTHUR HARRY and JOHN
The Knowle

GRANDMA and MAUREEN
at The Knowle

AUNTY MAY

Leah, Aunty and Mum

Olive, George, Monica, Aunty and Norman

JEAN VIV MONICA and PETER

JEAN and MONICA
23 London Road

White Horse Inn 1954

Jean's moulting jacket

JEAN and PEGGY
Hol's 1—Torquay

JEAN and JOY
Hol's 2—Belgium

Lightning Source UK Ltd.
Milton Keynes UK
08 January 2011

165390UK00001B/10/P